The New Vegetarian Cookbook

This edition published by
Barnes & Noble, Inc.,
by arrangement with
The Orion Publishing Group Ltd
1998 Barnes & Noble Books

M 10 9 8 7 6 5 4 3 2 1
ISBN 0-7607-1146-1

First published in 1996 by
George Weidenfeld & Nicolson Ltd
The Orion Publishing Group
Orion House
5 Upper St Martin's Lane
London WC2H 9EA

Designed by Bridgewater Books
Edited by Gillian Haslam
Colour photography by Gus Filgate
Black & white photography by Phil Starling
Styling by Penny Markham
Home Economy by Louise Pickford

I would like to thank Chris Curry and Gavin
Heys, respectively Chairman and Managing
Director of Cranks. I would also like to thank
Suzanne Cullen for her contribution to some
of the recipes.

My heartfelt thanks once again go to Sujan
who so efficiently and tirelessly supported and
assisted me throughout.

Special thanks to Gus Filgate, Louise Pickford
and Penny Markham for their unparalleled
artistry.

Finally, I would like to thank Beth Vaughan
and Laura Washburn at Weidenfeld & Nicolson
and Gillian Haslam, my editor, for her
encouragement and support when things
threatened to get on top of me.

Nadine Abensur

The New Vegetarian Cookbook

NADINE ABENSUR

BARNES & NOBLE BOOKS
NEW YORK

contents

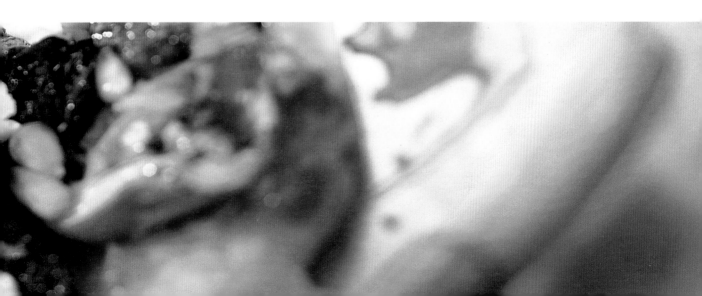

Vegetarian food has been at the heart of a culinary revolution over the past few years. The driving force behind this change is a public less rigidly attached to eating meals that center around meat. A more health-conscious, worldly attitude now informs the eating habits of just about everyone. The influence of other continents–Asia and the Middle East as well as the cooking of the Mediterranean–have had much to do with this.

introd

In the cooking of all these cultures, vegetables play a vital role, and a meal is often composed of several smaller courses, giving wider scope for imaginative use of ingredients, notably vegetables. With the increase in travel between countries has come a greater openness to external influences. Until very

recently most supermarkets offered no more than basic staples:

root vegetables in winter, strawberries in summer and, of

course, a bountiful supply of potatoes all year round. Local

grocers offered an even more limited range. Now, it is possible

to buy garlic, several varieties of lettuce, tomatoes and bell

peppers, just about anywhere,

any time of the year.

uction

In addition, contemporary travel

and food writers, television

shows devoted to cooking and

food magazines with vast circulations are helping to make food

exciting and accessible. The public at large,

after years in the wilderness, is experiencing

food and cooking in a totally different way.

They have seen and tasted and now want to

cook exciting food for themselves. Cookbooks

are selling in unprecedented numbers and it is

the new-found appreciation of vegetables that is the key to making modern cooking a fresh and lively art. It is as if we are waking from a deep sleep and are seeing for the first time a rainbow-colored display of vegetables. Nightmare memories of overboiled potatoes and soggy greens are over.

Supermarkets buy up entire fields to grow crops at home and abroad. Some food enthusiasts argue in favor of home-grown produce and seasonality, yet we hunger for variety and for the produce which, when out of season, we must seek from sunnier climes. The seasonality question will continue to be debated. But having acquired a taste for the exotic, we are not likely to hurry back to seasonal rationing. We will fearlessly experiment and explore, trying flavors that would have cowed us not so long ago.

More people are taking cooking classes, eager to acquire the skills which were lost as long ago as our grandmother's generation. An increasing number of us are now far more aware of what we eat and its effect on our health. We now know that more fruit and vegetables are essential for a healthy diet. And

there is increasing discomfort about modern animal husbandry,

with the factory rearing of livestock. As a result we are being

more adventurous and replacing more of our meals with

vegetarian options.

So now's the time for a new cookbook, from an English

restaurant chain called Cranks. Here you will find dozens of

ways to prepare vegetarian meals: Some are very simple and

others more sophisticated. In the chapter on main courses, you

will find the simpler recipes at the beginning and the more

sophisticated ones further on. You will discover new

combinations and seasonings, and we hope you will be inspired

to create some concoctions of your own.

For over 35 years a restaurant chain called Cranks has been the leader in changing Britain's views on vegetarian food, and its story in many ways reflects the prevailing culture of the times. Once regarded as "cranky"—hence the name—vegetarian food is now becoming accepted as mainstream.

the

In the early sixties, Cranks was not only at the center of burgeoning new values, it helped to establish them. Founded by husband and wife team David and Kay Canter and their friend Daphne

philos

Swann, Cranks quickly became known for its radical approach to food and service and its fresh decor. Just out of the fifties and with war rationing still fresh in the collective British memory, the attitudes of David, Kay, and Daphne were little short of revolutionary. Salad once meant nothing but iceberg lettuce, thick-skinned cucumber, and tasteless tomatoes doused with insipid bottled dressings. Salads from Cranks were bowlfuls of colorful, fresh vegetables, artfully combined and deliciously dressed. This was a stunning change.

Years before it became popular, Cranks zealously sourced organically grown, stone-ground flours and, against difficult odds, used organically grown vegetables whenever possible. They searched for and found an artisan dairy to produce additive-free yogurt and ice cream.

sophy

Meanwhile, a culinary revolution was taking place—new kitchen and diet aesthetics were being formed. Food was gradually becoming lighter and more delicate, and in contrast, traditional vegetarian food cooking seemed dull, heavy and—more than anything—brown. At the same time, large numbers of people began to realize that smart eating is one of the most important ingredients for good health.

In addition, the extraordinary influence of what is now known as the "Mediterranean Diet"—a diet rich in vegetables and polyunsaturated fats—came to the fore. Supermarkets now boast many types of olive oil and a bounteous variety of previously "exotic" produce, such as eggplants, all year round. Whatever anyone thinks about the burgeoning popularity of olive oil, there's no doubt that the general public is much more sophisticated, demanding of quality, and receptive to foods that are seen as first, delicious, and then as vegetarian. A new public has emerged and is making increasing demands on vegetarian cooking.

Thirty five years later, Cranks is still passionate about providing delicious, healthy, vegetarian food. We still use natural ingredients. Our meals are always additive-free, and always vegetarian. We are now using white, unbleached flour in certain recipes, but this is still organic. Our eggs still come from free-range chickens.

Vegetarian cooking has made huge strides. Improbable combinations such as lentil lasagne has been replaced with lighter, brighter alternatives. Where there was once a perceived need to replace or imitate meat, vegetables are now used with no apologies. The menu still consists of some of the old favorites such as Homity Pie, a delicious gratin of mashed potatoes, peas and cheddar cheese, which is still on the menu after 35 years

(there was such an outcry in the weeks when alternatives were

proposed); and besides, it is delicious. But now, it may appear side

by side with Polenta with Roasted Vegetables or Pasta with

Sundried Tomatoes, Broccoli, and Black Olives, or Noodles with

Pumpkin and Cilantro in Coconut Sauce. Next to the fruit bars

may sit a Pear and Almond Tart, and next to the legendary Carrot

Cake, a Lemon Tart made with oodles of heavy cream. Light or

rich, you can eat as you like.

appetizers

An appetizer is quite literally an entry into a meal. It calms the hunger and whets the appetite. In this chapter, the recipes range from an elegant feta cheese soufflé with sundried tomato paste to a robust Spanish omelet.

It is virtually impossible to serve a main course for more than one or two people without assistance or without ending up with cold food, but this first course is a completely different story. A cold appetizer can be arranged in advance, made to look picture perfect, and still allow you time to be with your guests.

Soups and salads make perfect appetizers, as do many of the vegetable dishes from the vegetable and side dishes chapter. Some of the recipes in this section are also ideal as main courses for lighter or summer meals. The rice-based recipes can all be made as individual timbales and served with a sauce or salsa. In fact, many of the savory recipes in this book can be adapted, by being served in smaller portions. So, when you have exhausted the recipes in this section, scour the other chapters for inspiration.

SPANISH POTATO OMELET

Spanish omelet, or at least a version of it, was a common meal in my childhood. It tended to have more vegetables than the recipe given here, and was baked in the oven. However, many years ago on a summer holiday to Cadaques in northern Spain, I witnessed the cooking of a dish which made me want to cook for the first time. While the rest of us impoverished foreign students ate from the campsite's none-too-promising facilities, the Spanish students were well equipped with their Calor gas stoves, their eggs and potatoes, their tomatoes and olive oil, and even their strings of garlic. And in front of our jealous eyes, they cooked a Spanish omelet like this (or as similar to this as I remember) every day.

SERVES
4 – 6

INGREDIENTS

- 1 cup light olive oil or a mixture of olive and corn oil
- 3 medium potatoes, peeled and thinly sliced
- 1 large onion, thinly sliced or diced
- 1 or more garlic cloves, crushed
- 8 eggs, medium sized, lightly beaten
- 3–4 tomatoes, diced
- salt and freshly ground black pepper

METHOD

Pour a little under half the olive oil into a large heavy-bottomed skillet. Add all the potatoes and onion, salt and pepper, and the crushed garlic, and cover with the rest of the oil. Cover with a lid and simmer very gently over low heat until the vegetables are tender. This will take at least half an hour. Don't allow the vegetables to brown in the slightest: The potatoes should be meltingly tender and quite waxy. Lift out with a slotted spoon and drain on paper towels, reserving the oil. Then beat the eggs and add the potatoes to them. Heat 3 tbsp of the reserved oil in the skillet on medium heat. Tip in the chopped tomatoes, and then the egg and potato mixture.

Cook until three-quarters set. The sides will go a rich golden brown. If you have a broiler, finish by browning the omelet under it. If not, cook a little longer in the pan. Allow to cool for a few minutes and invert. Eat hot or cold.

MANGO, PAPAYA, AND AVOCADO SALAD

WITH CRUMBLED DOLCELATTE

AND ORANGE AND RASPBERRY DRESSING

I particularly enjoy food which balances the five tastes: Sweet, salt, bitter, hot, sour. This salad should, of course, be eaten in the tropics but spoiled as we are, we may enjoy it on a warm sunny day. Use the very best fruit you can find.

INGREDIENTS

- 1 fragrant mango
- 1 ripe papaya
- 1 avocado
- ¼ lb pineapple flesh
- 1 scant handful fresh cilantro
- ½ cup raspberries, reserving 5–6 to crush into the dressing
- ½ cup Dolcelatte, gorgonzola, or other mild, creamy, blue-veined cheese, crumbled

- ½ cup blueberries
- ½ cup shelled walnuts, preferably fresh
- freshly ground black pepper

FOR THE DRESSING

- 3 tbsp olive oil or walnut oil
- 1 cup fresh orange juice
- 1 heaping tsp grain mustard

METHOD

Cut the mango, papaya, avocado, and pineapple into even-sized cubes and mix together with the cilantro and black pepper. Mix the dressing ingredients together with the reserved raspberries, and add to the salad. Scatter the cheese, raspberries, blueberries, and walnuts on top and serve at once.

EGGPLANT AND
WILD RICE GATEAU

Pasta, potatoes, rice; all can be set with egg in this way to make various versions of fritatas and tortillas, and what has ubiquitously come to be known as Spanish Omelet.

SERVES
8–10

INGREDIENTS

- 2 cups short-grain organic brown rice
- ½ cup wild rice
- ½ cup olive oil
- 2 cups onions, diced
- 2–3 garlic cloves, crushed
- 2 lbs canned tomatoes, drained and chopped
- 1 large sprig fresh basil
- 1 sprig fresh marjoram, oregano, or thyme
- 1½ lb eggplant, cut into ½ in slices
- dash of Tabasco

- 1¼ cups Cheddar cheese, shredded
- 4 eggs, medium sized, beaten
- ½ cup rolled oats
- 1 tbsp chopped basil
- 1 lb tomatoes, sliced and seasoned with salt, pepper, garlic, and Tabasco
- salt and freshly ground black pepper

METHOD

Cook the brown rice with the wild rice until tender (see recipe for Rice and Zucchini Timbales, page 23). In the meantime, heat a little less than half the olive oil and sauté the onion and garlic until transparent. Add the drained and chopped canned tomatoes, as well as the basil sprig and marjoram, and simmer for 15–20 minutes until further reduced to make a thick sauce.

Meanwhile, baste the eggplant slices with the remaining olive oil and sprinkle with a little salt and a dash of Tabasco. Place under a hot broiler until golden brown on both sides. Set aside.

Remove the wilted herbs from the tomato sauce. Mix the rice with the shredded cheese, tomato sauce, beaten eggs, rolled oats, and the chopped basil. Mix well and set aside.

Preheat the oven to 400°F. Very lightly oil a cake pan or round foil container 9 in in diameter and line with most of the eggplant slices. Then press down about half the rice mixture so it reaches halfway up the pan. Add the remaining eggplant slices and the tomato slices. Add the rest of the rice, again making sure that it is well pressed down.

Bake for 35–40 minutes or until firm. Let cool for a few minutes, then run a sharp knife around the edge, and invert onto a large plate. Eat hot or cold.

RICE AND ZUCCHINI TIMBALES

Substantial enough to make a meal with little more than a mixed salad, these timbales are popular at Cranks. The most important thing, as in all recipes which call for brown rice, is to cook the rice properly. The rice needs to be rinsed first, then covered with one and a half times its volume in water, and brought to a boil. The heat is then reduced and the rice simmered for 45 minutes, covered with a lid, until all the water is absorbed and the rice is tender. Some, in the pursuit of health, seem to think that brown rice should be al dente: Please let that be another wholefood misconception to bite the dust. You may add a little tamari or sea salt to the boiling water if you like.

INGREDIENTS

- 1 cup short-grain Italian, organic brown rice
- 1 tbsp corn oil
- ¼ cup onion, diced
- ¾ cup carrots, cut into a julienne
- 2–3 garlic cloves, crushed
- ¾ cup zucchini, cut into a julienne
- 1 tbsp sesame seeds

- 1 tbsp tahini
- 1 tsp cumin
- dash of Tabasco
- 1 tbsp parsley, finely chopped
- 1 tbsp cilantro leaves, finely chopped
- salt and freshly ground black pepper

METHOD

Bring the rice to a boil as described above. Meanwhile, heat the corn oil and sauté the onion until transparent. Add the carrots and half the garlic, and sauté for no more than 1 minute. Remove from the pan and sauté the zucchini together with the remaining garlic and sesame seeds for no more than 30 seconds. Add the tahini, cumin, Tabasco, parsley, cilantro, and seasoning to the cooked rice, then the carrots, and finally half the zucchini. Divide the reserved zucchini between six molds, 3 inches in diameter, and press down gently with your fingers. Press the rice mixture firmly onto the zucchini and invert. Eat warm or cold, with a mixed salad.

DEEP-FRIED WONTONS

WITH GREEN BEANS AND ASPARAGUS
IN BLACK BEAN SAUCE

Fresh wonton skins can be bought in Chinese supermarkets.
This dish also works well as a main course.

SERVES

6

INGREDIENTS

- 4 cups corn oil
- 1½ cups leeks, finely sliced
- 1 medium carrot, shredded
- 1 medium zucchini, shredded or cut into julienne
- 1 scallion, finely sliced
- ½ cup bean curd, crumbled and soaked in 2 tbsp hot water and ½ tsp bouillon powder
- 2 garlic cloves, finely crushed
- 1 piece shredded ginger, to taste
- 1 in piece chili pepper, finely chopped
- ½ tsp ground coriander
- dash of Tabasco
- ¼ tsp black bean sauce
- ½ cup whole almonds, lightly toasted and chopped
- 2 tsp lime juice
- pinch of nutmeg
- 18 wonton skins
- salt and freshly ground black pepper

TO SERVE

- 1 tbsp corn oil
- ½ red bell pepper. diced into ¼ in pieces
- ½ yellow bell pepper, diced into ¼ in pieces
- Tabasco
- 1 lb green beans, blanched in salted water for 5 minutes
- ¼ lb asparagus, 5 in long, blanched in salted water for 5 minutes
- 2 tbsp black bean sauce
- ½ cup water, reserved from blanching the vegetables

METHOD

Heat 1 tbsp of the oil in a pan and sauté the sliced leeks for 1 minute until transparent. Add the shredded carrot, zucchini, and scallion, and the drained tofu. Add the garlic, ginger, chopped chili, and ground coriander, and continue to fry for 1–2 minutes. Add a dash of Tabasco and the black bean sauce. Season with salt and pepper and remove from heat. Add the almonds, which should be chopped quite small but not as smooth as commercial ground almonds and still include some bigger pieces, and the lime juice and nutmeg. Let cool slightly, then work with your fingers for a few seconds until the ingredients are well mixed together. Shape into 18 equal-sized balls.

Lay out the wonton squares and place a ball of mixture on the center of each. Moisten the edges all the way round with a little water, using your fingers or a pastry brush. Bring the four corners up to meet in the middle and press the sides together so you end up with a pointed four-cornered purse.

Line a colander with at least two layers of paper towels. Heat the remaining oil in a pan until hot and gently drop in the filled wontons, three or four at a time. Sauté for 2 minutes until golden brown all over. You may need to turn them around with two forks and to hold them down as they tend to fall on one side and stay that way. Remove from the oil and immediately transfer to the colander to drain.

For the green beans and asparagus, heat half the oil and quickly sauté the diced red and yellow bell peppers, with just a little salt and pepper and a dash of Tabasco, and set aside. Heat the rest of the oil in the same pan and sauté the blanched green beans and asparagus for a minute or two. Add the black bean sauce and the reserved blanching water. Stir and sauté on high heat for 2 minutes, adding a dash of Tabasco, until the liquid is half reduced but be sure there is enough sauce to coat the vegetables generously. Return the red and yellow bell peppers to the pan and sauté for a further 30 seconds. Divide the green bean mixture between 6 plates, place 3 wontons on each, and serve.

SPINACH AND SUNDRIED TOMATO ROULADE

WITH CREAM CHEESE
AND FLAKED ALMOND FILLING

This is the ideal appetizer to make for a dinner party as the result is very impressive, and it can easily be made in advance.

INGREDIENTS

- 12 eggs, medium sized, separated
- 1¼ cups frozen spinach, thawed and squeezed of excess water
- 2 garlic cloves, crushed
- pinch of nutmeg
- 2 tbsp very red sundried tomato paste
- salt and freshly ground black pepper

FOR THE FILLING

- 1 tbsp almond flakes, lightly toasted
- 1 tbsp chives, finely chopped
- 1 cup low-fat cream cheese

METHOD

Prepare a baking tray 16 x 14 in by lining it with waxed paper, generously spread with butter. Preheat the oven to 325°F.

Place 6 egg yolks in one bowl and 6 in another, and set the whites aside. Add the drained spinach, a little salt, pepper, crushed garlic, and nutmeg to one bowl and the sundried tomato paste to the other. Whisk the egg whites in a separate bowl until they are stiff and stand in peaks and divide equally between the two bowls. Fold in gently with a metal spoon until well incorporated. Spread the spinach mixture along the whole length and half the width of the tray, and then spread the tomato mixture along the other half so you end up with two parallel strips. Place immediately in the preheated oven for 14 minutes, or until set. Let cool.

Meanwhile, make the filling by adding the almond flakes and chives to the cream cheese. Place a piece of plastic wrap larger than the roulade itself onto a clean work surface and invert the roulade onto it. When it is completely cold, spread the cream cheese mixture carefully over it with a spatula, leaving a ½ in gap around the edges as the filling will spread as you roll the roulade. Roll up gently from one long side as you would a Swiss roll.

To serve, trim both ends so that all three colors show, and slice. The roulade can be kept tightly wrapped up in plastic wrap in the fridge for up to 2 days.

RAVIOLI

WITH THREE FILLINGS IN
ROSEMARY, GARLIC, AND LIME BUTTER

I have given this as an appetizer recipe, only because making sufficient pouches for a main course may seem daunting. But by doubling the recipe, you will have quite enough for a dinner party for 6. The pouches are a full 2 inches in diameter by the time the edges have been pressed out so 3 each for an appetizer is sufficient.

A thin wooden rolling pin does the job of rolling best of all, and you do not need to use a pasta machine. I used mine just once and it has been sitting at the back of a cupboard ever since.

INGREDIENTS

FOR THE PASTA
- 3 cups bread flour
- 3 eggs, large
- 2 tbsp milk

FOR THE FILLINGS
- ¾ cup ricotta, drained in a sieve overnight
- ⅛ cup matzo meal or fine bread crumbs
- 1½ tsp freshly shredded Parmesan cheese
- 1 clove garlic, crushed
- ½ cup reconstituted dried mushrooms, chopped and sautéed in ½ tsp butter

- ⅛ lb arugula, wilted in ½ tsp heated butter for 30 seconds
- 3–4 asparagus spears, blanched and roughly chopped into small pieces

FOR THE ROSEMARY BUTTER
- ¾ cup butter
- 1 shallot, very finely diced
- 2–3 garlic cloves, crushed
- zest and juice of ½ lime
- 1 large sprig rosemary, leaves stripped

METHOD

To make the pasta, pile the flour onto the work surface and make a well in the center. Lightly whisk the eggs and 1 tbsp milk in a bowl and slowly pour into the well, gradually drawing in the flour with your hands until it is all absorbed. Then knead the dough for 8 minutes to form a smooth ball. Finally, divide the ball into two, wrap each half with plastic wrap, and let rest for 30 minutes.

To make the fillings, divide the ricotta into 3 equal amounts and add the equally divided matzo meal or bread crumbs, the Parmesan and garlic to each. Then add the mushrooms to one, the rocket to the second, and the asparagus to the third.

Allowing yourself plenty of space to work in, lightly flour the work surface. Roll out two pieces of pasta dough of equal size, side by side (you may need to start with pieces smaller than the original two balls) using a well-floured, thin wooden rolling pin.

Turn the pasta dough one quarter turn after each application of the rolling pin. Work in one direction only, rolling away from yourself, so that you are not so much rolling out the pasta as pushing it and stretching it away from you. Lift the pasta occasionally to make sure that it is not sticking to the surface and add a little more flour if necessary. The pasta, when rolled to the correct thickness, should be as thin as a silk scarf.

Place teaspoons of the fillings at equal intervals on one sheet of pasta, using a round cookie cutter 2 inches in diameter to help you mark out the gaps. Do not cut all the way through the pasta at this stage. Brush a little of the remaining milk around each circle.

Lift the second piece of pasta with the rolling pin and lay carefully on top of the first. Press down around the filling, with the milk helping to seal the two sheets of pasta together. Now cut out with the pastry cutter. Lift each pouch from the work surface and, with lightly floured fingers, press the edges even closer together so that the edges are barely thicker than the single layered centers. Lay on lightly floured plastic trays or boards lined with parchment paper.

To cook the pasta pouches, bring a large pan of salted water to a boil. Drop the pouches in one at a time but working quickly. Cook for 3–4 minutes, testing that they are tender before removing them with a slotted spoon.

For the rosemary butter, melt the butter and add the finely diced shallot and crushed garlic. Whisk quickly with a fork or small hand whisk for few seconds and then add the lime zest, juice, and rosemary. Stir again for a few seconds. Place 3 ravioli on each plate, pour the rosemary butter over, and serve.

GATEAU DE CREPES FLORENTINES

A colorful and easy recipe that is good hot or cold: Perfect as a summer's lunch and equally at home on a party buffet. Almost any combination of sauces works but always have 3. The crêpes should be fine and lacy. You actually need only 7 crêpes for one gâteau, but the recipe is for 12 because I know it is practically impossible to resist eating 1 or 2 as you go along.

SERVES
12

INGREDIENTS

FOR THE CREPES

- 1½ cups all purpose flour, sifted
- 2 eggs, large
- 1¼ cups milk, low-fat or full fat
- ½ cup water
- 2 tbsp olive oil
- pinch of salt

METHOD

Mix all the ingredients except 1 tbsp of olive oil together in a blender and blend thoroughly. Let stand for 2 hours.

Oil the bottom of a crêpe pan or other shallow, cast-iron pan with a piece of paper towel dipped into oil (you can use a non-stick frying or pancake pan but these don't tend to have a very long shelf life). Heat until a spoonful of the mixture dropped onto the pan sizzles immediately.

Pour in one small ladleful of the batter and tip the pan all around so that the batter covers it completely. Cook until golden brown underneath, then turn or toss over, and cook on the other side. Slide the crêpe onto a plate and repeat, oiling the pan in between each, until all the batter is used up.

INGREDIENTS

FOR THE EGGPLANT FILLING

- 1 large eggplant, cut into ¼ in slices
- 2 tbsp olive oil
- dash of Tabasco
- dash of balsamic vinegar
- 2 garlic cloves, crushed
- salt

FOR THE PEA-FENNEL FILLING

- 1 cup petits pois
- 3 tbsp butter
- 1 fennel bulb, cut into 1 in chunks
- 2 garlic cloves, crushed
- 1 tsp bouillon powder mixed with 6 tbsp hot water
- ¼ cup all purpose unbleached flour

- ¼ cup milk
- ¼ cup heavy cream
- salt and freshly ground black pepper

FOR THE TOMATO-OLIVE FILLING

- 3–4 tbsp olive oil
- 1 large onion, diced
- 1 lb can tomatoes, drained
- 2 garlic cloves, crushed
- several leaves of basil
- ¾ cup black olives, pitted

FOR THE TOPPING

- ¼ cup freshly shredded Parmesan cheese
- 1 tbsp finely chopped herb of your choice

METHOD

For the eggplant filling, baste the eggplant slices with olive oil and season with salt, Tabasco, and balsamic vinegar. Place under a hot broiler and brown on both sides for 4–5 minutes. Remove from heat and immediately sprinkle over the crushed garlic, taking care not to break up the slices in the process. Set aside.

For the pea-fennel filling, place the petits pois in a pan of boiling salted water and blanch for 3–4 minutes. Remove from the heat and refresh under cold water. Melt the butter in a pan and sauté the fennel with the crushed garlic. Add the bouillon, cover with a lid, and simmer gently for 4–5 minutes until the fennel is braised and soft. Add the petits pois and then sprinkle the flour over. Stir carefully until the flour is all absorbed. Add the milk and stir until the mixture thickens. Bring to a boil, stirring constantly, and finally add the cream, stirring for a couple of minutes. Season and set aside.

To make the tomato filling, heat the olive oil and sauté the onion until transparent. Add the drained tomatoes, garlic, and basil leaves. Reduce for about 15 minutes, stirring regularly. Add the black olives. At the last minute, remove the basil leaves.

Preheat the oven to 350°F. Lightly oil a round ovenproof dish and place one crêpe in it. Assemble the gâteau, alternating crêpes with the different fillings, until they are all used up. Finish with a crêpe. Cover with foil and bake for 10–15 minutes until hot. Invert onto a large plate. Sprinkle with Parmesan and finely chopped herbs, and wait a few minutes before cutting to allow the gâteau to settle.

COUSCOUS TERRINE

WITH BROILED RED PEPPERS AND EGGPLANT

The couscous for this terrine needs to be stickier than a normal light and fluffy couscous, hence the greater quantity of water given in this recipe. Serve with lime and cilantro cream (see page 110).

SERVES

6

INGREDIENTS

- ½ vegetable bouillon cube
- 4 cups boiling water
- 1¾ cups couscous
- 2 medium eggplants, sliced
- 3 tbsp olive oil
- 1 large onion, diced
- 1 large handful cilantro, chopped
- 1½ tsp mustard seeds

- ½ tsp grain mustard
- 2 garlic cloves, crushed
- 1 piece chili pepper, very finely chopped
- 3–4 tomatoes, juice and seeds removed and roughly chopped
- 2 red bell peppers, charbroiled, skin, pith, and seeds removed, and quartered (see page 173)
- salt and freshly ground black pepper

METHOD

Dissolve the bouillon cube in the boiling water, pour over the couscous and set aside for about 10 minutes.

Preheat the broiler. Baste slices of eggplant with some of the olive oil and a little salt and place under the hot broiler for 5 minutes, turning halfway through the cooking time. Set aside.

Heat the remaining olive oil in a pan and sauté the onion until soft. Add the fried onion to the couscous, together with the cilantro, mustard seeds, grain mustard, garlic, the chopped chili pepper, and tomatoes and further seasoning.

Line a 9 x 5 in loaf pan with plastic wrap so it hangs over the edges. Line the base with slices of broiled eggplant. Then press half the couscous firmly on top and add another layer of eggplant and the quartered broiled red bell peppers. Press the remaining couscous on top. Bring the overhanging plastic wrap over the top and refrigerate for 30 minutes.

Invert onto a large plate. Use a finely serrated knife to cut slices no thicker than 1 in and serve with a choice of salads.

EGGPLANT CHARLOTTE

This makes a highly effective dish for a buffet table, but its stunning appearance belies its extraordinary ease of preparation. Simply ensure that the eggplant slices are well browned and the tomato sauce well reduced, and garnish with fresh cilantro leaves.

SERVES
8

INGREDIENTS

- thick tomato sauce (see page 100)
- 1 tbsp sundried tomato paste
- 2 large eggplant
- ¼ cup olive oil
- ¼ cup Greek yogurt
- ¼ cup sour cream
- 3 garlic cloves, crushed
- pinch of nutmeg

- 1 large handful cilantro, roughly chopped, plus 1 large handful for garnish
- 1 large handful parsley, roughly chopped
- mixture of salad leaves such as sorrel, arugula, young romaine, oak leaf, and cilantro
- ¼ cup walnut oil
- salt and freshly ground black pepper

METHOD

Preheat the oven to 350°F. Mix the tomato sauce and sundried tomato paste, and set aside.

Slice the eggplants into ½ in slices, baste with olive oil, and bake in the oven for about 20 minutes, turning over halfway through the cooking time, until golden brown on both sides. Alternatively, place the basted slices under a hot broiler for 5 minutes, turning them over so that both sides brown.

Mix the yogurt, sour cream, garlic, nutmeg, fresh herbs, and salt and pepper.

Line the base of a round ovenproof dish with one-third of the eggplant slices. Then top with the tomato sauce, another layer of eggplant, then the yogurt and cream mixture, and end with eggplant slices. Bake in the preheated oven for 30–35 minutes then set aside to cool.

Toss the salad leaves with the walnut oil and seasoning. Run a knife around the sides of the charlotte and invert onto a large round plate, abundantly garnished with the salad leaves. Separate the remaining cilantro leaves from their stalks and press onto the charlotte's surface. Serve with chunks of ciabatta bread, riddled with sundried tomato.

SPINACH RISOTTO PIE

If you are a risotto fan, as I am, but cannot quite handle it as a summer meal, then try this baked risotto which is just as delicious eaten cold.

INGREDIENTS

- ½ cup bouillon powder
- 4 cups boiling water
- ¼ cup olive oil
- I cup onions, diced
- 3 garlic cloves, crushed
- pinch of nutmeg

- 2 cups Arborio rice
- I lb fresh spinach
- I cup Parmesan cheese, freshly shredded
- 6 eggs, medium sized, beaten
- I–2 tomatoes, cut into slices
- salt and freshly ground black pepper

METHOD

Preheat the oven to 400°F.

Make a stock with the bouillon powder and boiling water and keep warm. Heat the oil and add the onion, garlic, and nutmeg. Sauté until the onions are transparent. Now add the rice and also sauté until transparent, stirring all the time. Add the stock gradually, stirring continuously, until it is all absorbed and the grains are creamy but still intact, for about 20 minutes. Add the spinach and stir until it is wilted. Finally add the Parmesan and then the beaten eggs.

Oil a round ovenproof dish and line with the tomato slices and season. Add the rice mixture and bake in the preheated oven for 20–25 minutes. Run a knife around the pie and invert. Eat hot or cold.

FETA CHEESE AND SUNDRIED TOMATO SOUFFLE

SPIKED WITH FRESH HERBS AND BLACK OLIVES

You get a lot of mileage out of an egg, as you'll see from this recipe, which puffs and puffs, yet at the same time stays rich and creamy with a wonderful melting texture. Since a soufflé is little more than white sauce (and everyone knows how to make white sauce!) with added yolks and whisked egg whites, there is no reason for fear. It may all look like magic: All that whisking of egg whites creating millions of air bubbles which expand during baking. A few tricks help: Add a drop of lemon juice to the egg whites to prevent them from splitting and separating, and follow the old adage of using a spotlessly clean dry bowl when whisking the egg whites. Be scrupulous about this. Also, do not remove the soufflé from the oven as soon as it has risen, but let it sit there for a few seconds first.

SERVES

6

INGREDIENTS

- 1½ cups milk
- ¾ cup unsalted butter
- ¾ cup all purpose flour
- ¾ cup young, moist feta cheese, crumbled
- 1–2 basil leaves, finely shredded
- 3 tbsp sundried tomato paste
- ¼ cup chopped, pitted black olives
- 2 garlic cloves, preferably cooked first and mashed to a purée
- 5 large egg yolks
- 9 large egg whites
- juice of ½ small lemon
- salt and freshly ground black pepper

TO LINE THE SOUFFLE DISH
- 1 heaping tbsp unsalted butter, softened
- ¼ cup Parmesan cheese, freshly shredded

Preheat the oven to 375°F and place a baking sheet in it. Generously butter the sides of a 6 cup soufflé dish and add the Parmesan. Shake it all around so that it sticks to the butter and discard any excess. Chill until needed.

To make the white sauce, bring the milk to a boil. Melt the butter in a saucepan without letting it brown. Add the flour and stir for 1 minute. Gradually add the hot milk to the butter and flour mixture, stirring all the time until you have a smooth white sauce.

Remove from the heat and cool for a few minutes, again stirring, this time to prevent a skin from forming. Add the crumbled feta cheese, basil, sundried tomato paste, olives, garlic, and the egg yolks. Whisk with a hand-held whisk for a few moments. Season with a little salt and pepper.

In another bowl, whisk the egg whites to very soft peaks, then add the lemon juice. Continue whisking to firm peaks. Whisk a quarter of these into the cheese sauce base, then fold in the rest using a rubber spatula. Use the spatula again to scoop the soufflé mixture carefully into the soufflé dish, then run it along the inside of the dish to create a slight gap between the mixture and the dish. Bake in the preheated oven for 35–40 minutes until well risen and golden. Serve and eat immediately.

soups

Nothing is more evocative of home cooking than a good soup. Recipes range from the prosaic mixed vegetable to the sophisticated wild garlic and blood orange, yet neither requires any great skill or complex technique.

When making soup, good ingredients are essential, and good stock is absolutely vital. Though it is possible to use ready-made stock, nothing quite parallels the subtleties of a home-made stock. For a light stock, use light colored vegetables such as celery (leaves and all), leeks, onions, carrots, garlic, and a handful of fresh parsley. For a dark stock add to these a handful of brown lentils, some field mushrooms, a little tamari, bay leaves, and other herbs of your choice. Cover completely with water and bring to a boil, then simmer gently for at least 1 hour, until all the vegetables are soft and every bit of flavor has been extracted from them. Though soups are often served as a first course, many soups can be described as "a meal in a bowl." Additions of cheese, croûtons, fresh herbs, and lightly sautéed diced vegetables all contribute to a nourishing and satisfying meal.

CURRIED PARSNIP SOUP

I suppose that this is the kind of combination for which the term Anglo-Indian is a perfect fit. If possible, use small parsnips with no trace of woodiness.

INGREDIENTS

- 1 fl oz corn oil
- 1 onion, diced
- 1 potato, peeled and diced
- 1 tbsp mild garam masala
- 1 tsp ground coriander
- seeds from 2 cardamom pods, crushed

- 2 lb parsnips, chopped into ½ in pieces
- 2–2½ quarts vegetable stock or water
- 1 garlic clove, left whole
- 1 cup heavy cream
- salt and freshly ground black pepper

METHOD

Heat the oil in a large saucepan and sauté the onion until transparent. Halfway through, add the diced potato and sauté until this is also transparent. Add the garam masala, ground coriander, and crushed cardamom seeds. Stir for 2–3 minutes, adding a little water to loosen the spices. Add the chopped parsnips and sauté for 3–4 minutes. Add half the stock or water and the peeled garlic clove and bring to a boil. Reduce the heat and simmer gently for about 15 minutes until the parsnips are tender when poked with a fork, then blend in an electric blender until absolutely smooth, and return to the pan. Add the rest of the stock or water and bring back to a boil. Stir in the heavy cream and heat to boiling point. Adjust the seasoning if necessary and serve.

CARROT SOUP

WITH LIME, CILANTRO, COCONUT, AND SPINACH

Bulky vegetables, such as carrots, can be turned into the creamiest soups with barely any additional cream as long as you use a good blender. I've added ground almonds, or you could use very finely ground cashew nuts, loosened with a little water to make cashew butter. Both make the soup rich and nutritious. I always make this kind of soup in a pressure cooker, only adding the nuts and seasoning at the end.

SERVES
6

INGREDIENTS

- 2 lb carrots, cut into 1 in slices
- 1 large onion, cut into quarters
- 1 tbsp bouillon powder
- 1 clove garlic, left whole
- ¼ cup ground almonds
- ¼ cup creamed coconut
- juice of 1 lime

- ½ lb fresh spinach
- Greek yogurt or crème fraîche
- fresh cilantro leaves
- chunk of fresh coconut, finely shaved (optional)
- salt and freshly ground black pepper

METHOD

Place the carrots in a pressure cooker with the onion, bouillon powder, peeled garlic clove, a little salt, and enough water to cover. Bring to a boil and then cook under gentle pressure for 10 minutes or until the carrots are tender. Remove the garlic clove, and pour the soup into a blender with the ground almonds. Blend until absolutely smooth.

Return to the heat and add the creamed coconut until it is dissolved, then the lime juice, and finally the spinach. Add a little water if the consistency looks too thick. Stir long enough for the spinach to wilt, and remove from heat.

Serve at once, topped with a dollop of Greek yogurt or sour cream, black pepper, cilantro leaves, and a few shavings of fresh coconut.

OLD-FASHIONED LENTIL SOUP

This soup is delicious when first made but even better the next day when the flavors have had time to develop. You could add a handful of fresh spinach at the end or a red bell pepper, charbroiled, peeled, and cut into thin strips (see page 173).

SERVES

6

INGREDIENTS

- 3 fl oz olive oil
- 1 large onion, diced
- 1 tsp cumin
- 3 medium carrots, chopped
- 1 medium potato, peeled and diced
- 2 cups brown lentils
- 3–4 garlic cloves, left whole

- 2¼ quarts vegetable stock or water
- 1–2 tbsp tamari
- dash of Tabasco
- small bunch parsley, finely chopped
- 1–2 scallions, finely sliced
- salt and freshly ground black pepper

METHOD

Heat 1 tbsp oil in a large heavy-bottomed saucepan and sauté the onion with the cumin until transparent. Then add the carrots and potato, and sauté for a couple of minutes. Add the lentils, peeled garlic cloves, and half the stock or water. Bring to a boil, then reduce the heat and simmer for 20 minutes or so, stirring occasionally to prevent the soup from sticking to the bottom. Add the rest of the stock or water, and continue to cook slowly for a further 20–25 minutes, until the lentils are tender and the soup quite substantial in appearance. Add the remaining olive oil, the tamari, Tabasco, and seasoning. Just before serving, stir in the parsley and scallions.

RED ONION SOUP

WITH TOASTED CHEESE FLOATS

I am a great fan of red onions and thought I was being original when I first made this soup. Then I looked through Louise Pickford's beautiful book, *The Inspired Vegetarian*, and there of course it was: Lodged in my memory from an earlier perusal no doubt, though our seasoning differs and I have retained the Gruyère of the original French recipe instead of Louise's goat's cheese for the toasts.

SERVES

6

INGREDIENTS

- 5 fl oz olive oil
- 3 lb red onions, thinly sliced
- 3–4 garlic cloves, crushed
- 1 tsp basil, chopped
- 1 tsp marjoram, chopped
- 1 bay leaf
- 6 fl oz marsala or port wine

- 1 quart dark vegetable stock (see page 42)
- 1–2 tbsp tamari
- salt and freshly ground black pepper

FOR THE CHEESE TOASTS

- 6 pieces of French bread, cut into ½ in slices
- ¾ cup Gruyère cheese, shredded

METHOD

Heat the oil in a pan and sauté the onions over medium heat for 25–30 minutes, stirring regularly to prevent the onions from sticking and burning. Add the garlic and the herbs, then most of the wine or port. Simmer to reduce the liquid by about half. Then add the stock and bring to a boil. Lower the heat, and simmer gently for a further 20 minutes. Add the remaining wine and the tamari, and simmer for another couple of minutes. Taste for seasoning.

Just before serving, prepare the toasts: Lay the bread under a broiler and toast lightly on both sides. Pile some of the shredded Gruyère onto one side. Pour the soup into heatproof bowls and place a toast in each bowl. Place the bowls under the broiler until the cheese is melted and golden brown. Serve at once.

CARIBBEAN PEPPERPOT

This is a very popular item on the Cranks menu. Garnished with peppers, the soup is vibrant, fragrant, and colorful.

INGREDIENTS

- 6 tbsp corn oil
- I cup onions, diced
- 3 garlic cloves, finely chopped
- 2 cups potatoes, peeled and cut into ¼ in dice
- ½ tsp bouillon powder, dissolved in
  1¼ cups hot water
- I cup white cabbage, diced
- 1¾ cups canned chopped tomatoes
- I heaping tbsp paprika
- I heaping tsp ground coriander
- dash of Tabasco

- ½ tsp chili powder
- I piece fresh chili pepper, finely chopped
- 2¼ cups coconut milk
- pinch of soft brown sugar (optional)

FOR THE PEPPERS

- I tbsp corn oil
- I red bell pepper, cut into ¼ in dice
- I yellow bell pepper, cut into ¼ in dice
- Tabasco
- 1–2 tbsp tamari

METHOD

Heat the oil and sauté the diced onion and garlic until transparent. Add the diced potatoes and cook until they too are transparent. Add 5 tbsp of the hot bouillon, stir, and cook for 1 minute or so. Then add the diced cabbage and sauté for 2–3 minutes. Drain the chopped tomatoes, reserving the juice. Add the tomatoes to the soup together with the paprika, ground coriander, Tabasco, and chili powder. Stir well and add a further ¾ cup of the hot bouillon, the reserved tomato juice, and the fresh chili pepper. Simmer gently for 7–8 minutes and add the coconut milk. Check the sweetness of the soup and, if necessary, add a pinch of soft brown sugar.

For the bell peppers, heat the oil in a skillet and sauté the diced bell peppers for just a minute, until they begin to blacken in places. Add a drop or two of Tabasco and tamari to taste, and set aside.

To serve, mix half the bell peppers into the soup and reserve the rest to use as garnish on each serving or in the soup tureen.

WILD MUSHROOM SOUP
WITH PORT

This recipe makes a small number of wild and dried mushrooms go a long way. It is a very rich soup and very elegant, the perfect appetizer for a dinner party.

SERVES
6

INGREDIENTS

- ¼ cup dried mushrooms
- 1 cup hot water
- ¼ cup butter
- 1 cup onions, diced
- 4 garlic cloves, crushed
- ¼ cup shiitake mushrooms, sliced

- ¾ cup mixed fresh wild mushrooms, gently brushed or wiped clean, then stalks trimmed
- ½ cup port
- 1 quart vegetable stock
- 1¼ cups heavy cream
- ½ tsp grain mustard
- salt and freshly ground black pepper

METHOD

Soak the dried mushrooms in the hot water for 30 minutes until reconstituted, and set aside. Drain the mushrooms, retaining the soaking liquid. Line a strainer with cheesecloth and pour through the soaking liquid to remove any grit, and set the liquid aside.

Place the butter in a saucepan and melt over gentle heat. Add the diced onion and sauté with the garlic until brown. Add the sliced shiitake mushrooms and sauté for a further 5–6 minutes. Now add the wild mushrooms and sauté again, stirring regularly, for another 3–4 minutes. Then add the soaked dried mushrooms and the strained soaking liquid, half the port, and some of the stock, and cook until reduced by about half. Then blend the soup in an electric blender until smooth and return to the pan.

Add the heavy cream and bring gently to a boil. Add the remaining port and continue to simmer for a couple of minutes. Finally, pour in the remaining stock, add the mustard, adjust the seasoning, stir well, and serve.

MINESTRONE

This is a textbook classic which has been adulterated in often far from flattering ways. The Cranks version is delicious, especially when served with Parmesan, and better still the next day when the flavors have had time to develop.

INGREDIENTS

- 4 tbsp olive oil
- I onion, diced
- 6 ripe tomatoes, peeled and chopped
- 4 medium potatoes, peeled and diced
- I quart vegetable stock
- I¼ cups shelled fava beans, fresh or frozen
- I cup petit pois, fresh or frozen
- I cup mushrooms, roughly chopped

- I¼ cups green beans, cut into small pieces
- I cup zucchini, diced
- I small cauliflower, broken into small flowerets
- I¾ cups canned cannellini beans, drained
- 4 tbsp parsley, finely chopped
- 2 cups small pasta shapes
- salt and freshly ground black pepper
- ¾ cup Parmesan cheese, freshly shredded

METHOD

Heat the oil in a pan and sauté the onion until transparent. Add the tomatoes, salt, and pepper, and sauté for a further 5 minutes. Now add the potatoes and half the stock. Bring to a boil and simmer until the potatoes are tender. Then add the fava beans, peas, mushrooms, green beans, zucchini, cauliflower, and the remaining stock, and simmer for about 25 minutes until the vegetables are very tender. Next, add the cannellini beans and heat through. Add the parsley and stir for 3–4 minutes. Bring to a boil, add the pasta, and boil for 10 minutes. Serve with the freshly shredded Parmesan.

BORSCHT

WITH ACCESSORIES

I have been served Borscht by Russians and by Poles, both of whom thought their version definitive. The Russian recipe, on which this is based, is thick, rich, and filling. I recall that it was served with vodka, icy cold and wild, which gave a mood of extreme jollity and made the experience more authentic.

INGREDIENTS

- 2 lb small fresh beets
- ¼ cup corn oil
- 1 large onion, diced
- 1 lb potatoes, peeled and diced
- ¾ cup carrots, chopped
- dash of Tabasco
- 3 garlic cloves, finely chopped
- ½ cup vodka
- juice of 1 small lemon or lime
- salt and freshly ground black pepper

TO GARNISH

- ¾ lb potatoes, peeled, part-boiled and diced
- 1 quart corn oil, for deep-frying
- ¾ cup Greek yogurt or sour cream
- 1 tbsp parsley, finely chopped
- 1 tbsp dill, finely chopped

METHOD

Wash and trim the beets and bring to a boil in a pan of salted water. Cook for about 45 minutes until tender but still firm. Remove from the cooking liquid and reserve this for later use. Slip off the skins and chop into quarters.

Heat the oil and sauté the onion until transparent and then add the diced potatoes, carrots, salt, pepper, Tabasco, and chopped garlic, and continue to sauté for about 5 minutes. Add the beets and cook for a further 2 minutes. Pour in the reserved beet cooking liquid and continue to simmer gently for about 10 minutes. Add the vodka and lemon or lime juice and remove from heat. Blend until smooth with a hand-held whisk and set aside.

For the garnish, be sure the potatoes are dry (drain on paper towels if necessary) and deep-fry in the heated corn oil. (Alternatively, boil the potatoes completely and dice, and omit the deep-frying.)

Serve the soup warm with a dollop of sour cream or Greek yogurt and some finely chopped herbs on each serving, with the potatoes on the side.

CREAM OF ONION SOUP

This delicious version of French onion soup comes from Bordeaux, but I have omitted the flour and obtained the same rich creamy texture simply by blending.

SERVES

6

INGREDIENTS

- ¼ cup butter
- 5 cups onions, diced
- 2–3 garlic cloves, crushed
- pinch of nutmeg
- 3 cups light vegetable stock (see page 42)

- 2 egg yolks
- ½ cup heavy cream
- I tsp lemon juice
- I tbsp chives, snipped
- salt and freshly ground black pepper

METHOD

Heat the butter in a large heavy-bottomed saucepan and sauté the onion and garlic together with salt, pepper, and nutmeg until soft and transparent. Add the stock and stir until it comes to a boil. Cover with a lid and simmer for 30 minutes, checking regularly that it is not sticking to the bottom. Let cool for a few minutes and blend until smooth.

In a bowl, beat the egg yolks and cream with the lemon juice and gradually add in a ladle of the hot soup. Slowly stir the egg yolk mixture back into the rest of the soup and heat through again, but do not let it boil. Garnish with snipped chives and serve.

COUNTRY VEGETABLE SOUP

Some people prefer chunky soups, where they can see what they are eating, while others prefer velvety smooth ones, such as this. Made in a pressure cooker and puréed in a blender, this soup–for all its ingredients–can be ready in 25 minutes.

The combination of vegetables is open to interpretation, and you can be more adventurous with the seasoning or finish off with heavy cream, but this recipe shows how good even a very simple soup can be.

SERVES

6

INGREDIENTS

- 4–5 medium carrots, chopped
- 1 large onion, cut in quarters
- 1 fennel bulb, trimmed and cut in quarters
- 1 cup oyster or open cap mushrooms, chopped
- 3 leeks, trimmed and chopped
- 1 medium zucchini, chopped
- 3 medium potatoes, peeled and chopped
- ½ small cauliflower, separated into flowerets

- 2 quarts water
- 1 tbsp bouillon powder
- bunch of basil
- 1 whole garlic head, cloves separated and left whole
- ¼ cup olive oil or 2 tbsp butter
- salt and freshly ground black pepper

METHOD

Place all the vegetables, the water, bouillon powder, basil, peeled garlic cloves, and seasoning in a pressure cooker and bring to pressure for 10 minutes. Reduce the heat and cook under pressure for a further 10 minutes. Let cool slightly and blend until smooth. Stir in the olive oil or butter, adjust the seasoning if necessary, and serve.

FRESH GARLIC AND BLOOD ORANGE VICHYSSOISE

WITH GARLIC LEAF AND CILANTRO

This is one of the most delicate and elegant soups going. Choose blood oranges with dark and shrivelled skins for a truly blood red juice, the effectiveness of which is truly surprising. The garlic itself is white with hints of pale green and comes apart in delicate folds of fine skin. Garlic leaf can be found in Oriental shops.

SERVES
6

INGREDIENTS

- 9 heads young fresh garlic, trimmed, and tough outer leaves removed
- 3 tbsp unsalted butter
- ½ lb new potatoes, peeled and diced into ¼ in cubes
- 1–1¼ quarts water

- 5–6 saffron strands
- juice from 4 blood oranges
- pinch of soft brown sugar (optional)
- handful fresh cilantro, roughly chopped
- 1 fresh garlic leaf, finely shredded
- salt and freshly ground black pepper

METHOD

Slice the prepared garlic very finely, as you would an onion or leek. Melt the butter in a heavy-bottomed saucepan and add the garlic. Simmer over gentle heat until transparent and add the diced potatoes. Continue to cook until these too are transparent. Add some of the water and the saffron strands, and continue to simmer gently for about 15 minutes, adding the rest of the water a little at a time as needed.

Blend in an electric blender until absolutely smooth, and pass through a strainer if necessary. Return to low heat and add the orange juice and sugar and salt to taste. Garnish with the roughly chopped fresh cilantro, finely shredded garlic leaf, and a little freshly ground black pepper. Serve at once. This soup can also be eaten cold.

CHICKPEA SOUP
WITH LIME-INFUSED CREAM

This is a rich, intense, spicy soup reminiscent of the Moroccan Harira, to which the lime cream is a welcome cooling agent. This and other bean-based soups are best made in a pressure cooker if time is a concern. Otherwise, cook the soup slowly over a period of 1½ hours, adding a little liquid each time you see it beginning to over-thicken.

INGREDIENTS

- 6 tbsp olive oil
- 1 large onion, diced
- 3 garlic cloves, finely chopped
- 1 tbsp cumin
- 6–8 cups water
- 1 tbsp paprika
- 2 cups dried chickpeas, soaked overnight
- 3 garlic cloves, left whole

- 1 large handful fresh cilantro, roughly chopped
- dash of Tabasco
- salt and freshly ground black pepper

FOR THE LIME CREAM

- zest and juice of 1 lime
- 2 cups Greek yogurt
- smattering of freshly ground nutmeg

METHOD

Heat 1½ tbsp of the olive oil in a pressure cooker. Then add the onion and chopped garlic, and sauté until transparent. Add the cumin and sauté for a minute, stirring all the time, and adding 2–3 tbsp of water as soon as the mix dries out. Continue in this way, adding the paprika and about ¾ cup of water.

Add the drained chickpeas, stirring until they are well coated in the spices. Finally add the rest of the water–about 6 cups–and the whole peeled garlic cloves. Bring to pressure, then reduce the heat to a slow simmer for 25 minutes. Test to see that the chickpeas are completely soft and about to fall apart. Add a little water if necessary, and continue to simmer uncovered for 8–10 minutes, adding the remaining olive oil at the same time. Also add salt at this stage.

To make the lime-infused cream, mix the lime zest and juice with the yogurt and allow to sit for 20–30 minutes. Stir in some fresh ground nutmeg.

Just before serving, add the cilantro, Tabasco, and pepper, to the soup and continue to simmer for just a couple more minutes. You can mash the soup with a potato masher so that some of it is smooth and some rough or you can blend it smooth, in which case you should wait until afterward to add the cilantro. Serve with the lime cream.

CREAM OF BROCCOLI SOUP
WITH WALNUT AND DOLCELATTE GNOCCHI

We often make broccoli and blue cheese soup at Cranks, and this is a more sophisticated way of presenting and serving it. The soup itself, if you make it in a pressure cooker, takes only 10 minutes, so it's worth making these mock gnocchi to add to it. Whatever you do, don't overcook the broccoli: It needs to be tender enough to blend easily, but don't cook out the bright forest green color.

INGREDIENTS

- 1 lb broccoli, cut into small flowerets
- ½ cup onions, diced
- ¾ cup potatoes, peeled and diced
- 1¼ quarts water
- 2 tsp bouillon powder
- 2 garlic cloves
- 5 tbsp heavy cream
- salt and freshly ground black pepper

FOR THE GNOCCHI

- 12 walnuts, shelled and crushed finely
- ¾ cup Dolcelatte cheese
- ½ cup ricotta
- 2 cups soft, fresh bread crumbs
- 1 egg, medium sized, beaten
- 3 tbsp toasted fine bread crumbs
- 1 quart corn oil, for deep-frying
- salt and freshly ground black pepper

METHOD

Place all the soup ingredients except the cream in a pressure cooker. Bring to a boil and simmer for 10 minutes. Blend until very smooth, then add the heavy cream. Adjust the seasoning and set aside.

For the gnocchi, mix walnuts into the cheeses, either with a fork or your hand, so it looks like a paste. Add all the soft, fresh bread crumbs.

Place the beaten egg in one shallow dish and the toasted bread crumbs in another. Shape the cheese mixture into small walnut-sized pieces and dip in the beaten egg, then in the toasted bread crumbs. Line a colander with several layers of paper towels. Heat the oil until it is very hot and deep-fry the gnocchi for a minute until they are golden and crisp on the outside. Remove to the colander to drain, then serve immediately with the soup.

main courses

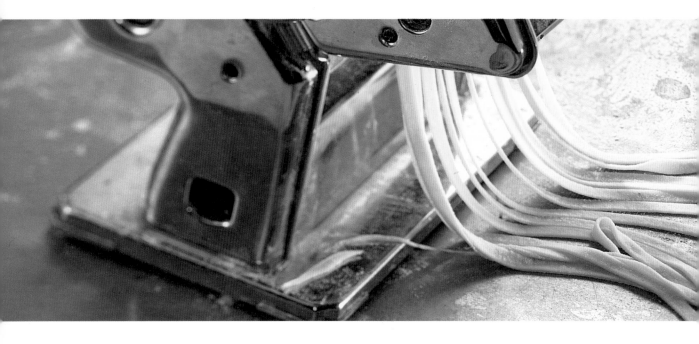

You won't find nut roasts and lentil stews in this chapter. Instead, experiment with mushroom fricassée with individual soufflés, or pumpkin with noodles and coconut cream, or vegetable brochettes with spiced rice.

I have never understood why main courses are thought to be the hardest part of a vegetarian meal. Perhaps the concept of meat and two vegetables is too hard to dispel. Yet many of the world's cuisines revolve around a selection of small dishes, with a mingling of flavors all complementing one another.

More formal occasions lend themselves to a meal with an identifiable centerpiece. It adds a sense of ceremony when there is something to cut into and share. More informal meals are wonderful ways for everyone to sample a little bit of this and a little bit of that, each playing on a different color or taste experience.

Then, of course, there is pasta which can be imaginative and delicious, whether served with charred vegetables, precious ingredients, or simple sauces: As basic or as sophisticated as you choose.

POTATOES WITH RED ONION AND TOMATOES

This is a slowly cooked potato dish that becomes melting and soft as the thin potato slices absorb the olive oil. For a robust and warming meal, serve with a substantial salad or side vegetable dish, or serve with Filled Eggplant Rolls (see page 82).

(see page 82).

SERVES

6

INGREDIENTS

- 4½ lb small potatoes
- ½ cup olive oil
- I garlic clove, crushed
- I red onion, cut into thin wedges
- 8 tomatoes, cut into quarters
- salt and freshly ground black pepper
- fresh basil leaves, to garnish

METHOD

Preheat the oven to 325°F.

Fill a large bowl with cold water. Peel the potatoes and instantly immerse them in the water to stop them going black. Cut into ⅛ in thick slices and pat the potato slices dry between two clean dish clothes.

Mix them thoroughly with the olive oil, salt, pepper, and crushed garlic, then pack closely into an ovenproof dish. Arrange the red onion and tomato slices, poking them down a bit on the top so that they are only partly exposed; they will burn if they are overexposed. Cover the dish with a lid or a piece of waxed paper (not foil, as this can react with the tomatoes and turn the whole dish black).

Bake in the preheated oven for 45–50 minutes. Remove the lid and turn the heat up to 400°F and bake for a further 10 minutes until the top layer is gently crisped. Serve hot, garnished with the basil.

TAGLIATELLE

WITH FAVA BEANS, SAFFRON, AND SUNDRIED VEGETABLES

Sundried eggplant, bell peppers, and zucchini can be found in specialty food stores. In their absence, slice half an eggplant into slices 1/8 in thick and a zucchini into slices just slightly thicker than that. Brush very lightly with olive oil and sprinkle with sea salt. Place in an oven set at its lowest heat and bake, or more accurately dry out, for 1–2 hours. Cut into thin strips and proceed.

*SERVES
6 – 8*

INGREDIENTS

- 2¼ cups fava beans, fresh or frozen
- 1½ lb green tagliatelle
- 5 fl oz olive oil
- 3 garlic cloves, finely sliced
- ½ lb sundried vegetables; mixture of zucchini and eggplant, and tomatoes in oil, all cut into thin strips

- 5–6 saffron strands, soaked in ¼ cup boiling water
- ¼–1 cup heavy cream
- several basil leaves
- ¾ cup Parmesan cheese, freshly shredded
- salt and freshly ground black pepper

METHOD

Blanch the fresh or frozen fava beans in salted water for 2 minutes, refresh quickly under cold water, and split the skins to slide out the bright green beans. Set aside.

Cook the tagliatelle in plenty of salted boiling water with the addition of 1 tbsp of the olive oil, which helps the pasta not to stick together. Turn the pasta once or twice with a fork to separate it, and when the water has returned to a boil, lower the heat so it does not boil over. When *al dente*, transfer to a large strainer or fine colander and run under cold water for a few seconds, separating the strands of pasta if necessary.

Heat the remaining olive oil in a large saucepan over gentle heat and add first the sliced garlic and, 30 seconds later, the sundried vegetables. Add the saffron stock. Simmer for 5 minutes or so, then add the tagliatelle and cream to taste. Bring to a gentle bubble and immediately add the shelled, blanched fava beans, stirring very gently for just as long as it takes to heat them through too.

Pour the tagliatelle and vegetables onto a large warmed pasta plate or bowl and add the basil and Parmesan. Toss and serve immediately.

PASTA WITH ARTICHOKE HEARTS, PINE NUTS, AND GREEN OLIVES

I use supermarket spiralli pasta, but the choice of pasta is pretty much up to you, although a heartier, fuller shape is preferable to a thinner, more delicate one.

SERVES
6

INGREDIENTS

- 6 small artichokes
- ¾ cup olive oil
- dash of Tabasco
- 2 garlic cloves, crushed
- 1 tbsp balsamic vinegar
- 1 lb spiralli pasta

- 1¼ cups green olives, sliced or left whole
- 1 cup pine nuts, lightly toasted
- handful of cilantro leaves, roughly chopped
- ¾ cup freshly shredded Parmesan cheese (optional)
- salt and freshly ground black pepper

METHOD

Prepare the artichokes by removing the outer leaves to reveal the purple and white ones, and trimming these to 1¼ inches in length. Peel the stem of all its fibrous and inedible outer layer, and then cut the artichokes in half across the length. Take out the choke and cut in half again, so you end up with each artichoke cut into quarters. Baste with some of the olive oil, salt, pepper, and Tabasco, then place under a hot broiler for about 20 minutes, turning over at least once in the process. Remove from the heat and marinate in a mixture of the remaining olive oil (reserving 1 tbsp), crushed garlic, and balsamic vinegar, for at least 1 hour.

Bring a large pan of salted water to a boil, add the reserved spoon of olive oil. Add the pasta, stirring once at the beginning to loosen it and prevent it sticking together. Lower the heat and cook, following packet instructions regarding timing. Drain and refresh briefly under cold water. Quickly return to the pan and add the artichoke hearts and the marinade, as well as the green olives. Heat through quickly, tossing the ingredients about, and finish off at the last moment with the pine nuts, cilantro, and seasoning to taste. Serve at once with the shredded Parmesan if desired.

PENNE WITH SUNDRIED TOMATO AND CREAM SAUCE

Sundried tomatoes are no longer a rarity. Their strong and distinctive flavor means that just a small amount cut into slivers can immediately elevate a dish from ordinary to sublime. Even more delicious is sundried tomato paste, which can be added to dressings and sauces, or spread on bruschetta or even plain ordinary toast, or whisked into ricotta to make a light mousse.

Some ready-made sundried tomato paste is bright red and slightly sweetened, which is no bad thing. If you make your own, adding a touch of sugar will round off the taste. Simply blend the contents of a jar of sundried tomatoes, including the oil they are preserved in, until very smooth.

SERVES
6

INGREDIENTS

- 1 lb penne
- 1 tbsp olive oil
- thick tomato sauce (see page 100)
- handful of basil
- ½ cup sundried tomatoes in oil, cut into thin slivers
- 1 cup sundried tomato paste
- 1 cup heavy cream
- salt and freshly ground black pepper

METHOD

Add the pasta to a pan of boiling salted water with the olive oil, and cook according to packet instructions until *al dente*. Remove from the heat, drain, and refresh.

Meanwhile, heat the tomato sauce in a large pan. Add half the basil, the sundried tomato slivers, and the sundried tomato paste. Briefly bring to a boil and add the heavy cream. Stir and bring to boiling point. Add the pasta and mix well. Serve immediately, garnished with the remaining basil and black pepper.

RICE AND VEGETABLE BIRYANI

I cannot vouch for the absolute authenticity of this dish. For a start, I use butter and olive oil instead of the more traditional ghee. It is just reminiscent of the kind of dish I ate in Kashmir many years ago. After eight months of living in India, the milder, sweeter, creamier dishes were manna. Rice and vegetable biryani makes a frequent and well-received appearance on the Cranks menu.

SERVES
4 – 6

INGREDIENTS

FOR THE VEGETABLE CURRY

- 2 tbsp butter
- 1 cup olive oil
- 2 cups onions, diced
- 4 cardamom pods, split and seeds pounded in a pestle and mortar
- 1 tbsp cumin
- 1 heaping tsp ground coriander
- 1 heaping tsp ground ginger
- ¼ tsp mustard seeds
- 3–4 cloves
- ¼ tsp dried fiery red chili peppers, finely chopped
- 4 garlic cloves, crushed
- 3 cups water
- 1½ cups potatoes, peeled and diced
- 1½ cups carrots, cut into slices, ½ in thick
- 3 medium tomatoes, quartered
- 1 lb cauliflower, trimmed and separated into small flowerets
- large pinch of saffron threads
- ½ lb small zucchini, cut into ½ in slices
- ½ cup coconut butter
- few drops of tamarind juice (optional)
- 1 bunch fresh cilantro, roughly chopped
- salt

FOR THE RICE

- 1¼ cups basmati rice
- 1 fl oz corn oil
- 1 cup onion, diced
- 1 tbsp mustard seeds
- 4 cardamom pods, split and seeds pounded in a pestle and mortar
- ½ cup raisins
- ½ cup chopped whole almonds
- pinch of saffron threads
- 1 piece fresh fiery red chili pepper, finely chopped
- 1 cup flaked coconut

FOR THE YOGURT TOPPING

- 2 cups plain yogurt
- 1 tbsp flaked almonds
- 1½ tsp flaked coconut
- zest of 1 lime
- 1 tbsp raisins

METHOD

Heat the butter and half the oil, and sauté the onion over medium heat for
8–10 minutes or until light brown. Add the cardamom, cumin, ground coriander,
ginger, mustard seeds, cloves, and finely chopped dried chili pepper. Sauté for a few
seconds, then add the crushed garlic and continue to sauté for 2 minutes, adding a little
of the water if necessary. Add the potatoes and sauté for 8 minutes. Then add the
carrots and half the tomatoes, which will dissolve to make a sauce.

Add the rest of the oil little by little from this point onward as you continue to cook
the curry. Add the cauliflower flowerets and continue to cook for 5 minutes, adding
more water as you go along (about ¾ cup each time) to prevent the vegetables from
sticking but making sure that it is all absorbed each time to maintain the curry's thick
and rich consistency. Then add the saffron, the zucchini slices, the coconut butter, and
tamarind juice, and stir until well combined. Continue to simmer for 20–25 minutes,
stirring frequently and adding a little more water from time to time. Finally, add the
rest of the tomato quarters and the fresh cilantro and fold in gently for just a couple of
minutes before serving.

Meanwhile, cook the basmati rice according to packet directions. In a separate pan,
heat the oil and sauté the onion until transparent. Add the mustard seeds and crushed
cardamom seeds, and continue to sauté for about 8 minutes until the onion is pale
golden brown. Add the raisins, almonds, saffron threads, finely chopped chili pepper,
and flaked coconut, and sauté for a further 5–6 minutes, stirring regularly. Finally add
the cooked rice and stir well so that the flavors mingle and the rice is speckled with the
orange hue of the saffron.

To assemble, preheat the oven to 375°F. Place the rice at the bottom of an ovenproof
dish and then pour the curry over it. Pour the yogurt on top and sprinkle with the
almonds, flaked coconut, lime zest, and raisins. Heat for 15–20 minutes so that the
yogurt sets slightly. Serve at once.

PIZZAS

When it comes to making bread and pizza doughs, I prefer to remain as old-fashioned and traditional as possible. There is no dried yeast and no food processor for me. I like the frothiness and the unmistakable smell of fresh yeast, and the kneading and stretching and general thumping of the dough. But I admit that this is pure romanticism and you could halve the preparation time by resorting to labor-saving devices.

This recipe makes six 4 inch pizzas. I prefer my pizza bases thin and crisp, so don't allow for a second rising. If you prefer a thicker, more focaccia-like base, you must allow the dough to rise for a further 20 minutes after rolling it out.

I have given three different toppings, but the frontiers of possibility can be pushed further: Try lettuce hearts or chicory, Gorgonzola, and pears (I had this in a pizzeria whose humble location belied the ingenuity of its menu and the devotion of its Italian staff). By far the most sublime of all is a pizza I ate from a stall in the old Jewish quarter of Rome. It had the thinnest of crispy bases brushed with the sweetest layer of tomato sauce, the creamiest of young buffalo mozzarella and, to my wonder, the most delicate and delicious layer of zucchini flowers, the color of an Impressionist sunshine. I do not include this recipe here, because unless you are of the rare breed who grow their own flowering zucchini, it is ruinously expensive. Still, if it's the thought that counts, know that a pizza, as well as being a jolly, work-a-day sort of meal, has aristocratic cousins and start planting the zucchini seeds.

INGREDIENTS

SERVES
6

FOR THE DOUGH
- 2 tbsp cake yeast
- ½ tsp sugar
- ¾ cup hand-hot water

- 2½ cups white bread flour
- I heaping tsp salt
- I tbsp virgin olive oil

METHOD

Dissolve the cake yeast with the sugar in a little of the water and set aside for about 10 minutes until a froth appears on the surface. Place the flour mixed with the salt in a mound on your work top or simply in a bowl and make a shallow well in the center. Pour the warm liquid into the well and mix with the flour. Then add the olive oil and the rest of the water. It is difficult to give an exact quantity of water so if the dough is too sticky, simply sprinkle a little more flour into it, and if it is too dry and does not hold together properly, add a little more water until the dough comes cleanly away from the work surface or bowl. Knead the dough on a lightly floured surface for 8–10 minutes until it is smooth and elastic.

Place in a lightly floured bowl and make an incision across the top with a knife, which will help it rise. Sprinkle a little more flour on top, cover loosely with a dish cloth and place in a warm, draft-free spot to rise until doubled in volume. This may take as little as 45 minutes or as long as 3 hours, depending on the temperature.

Punch down the dough, adding a little flour if necessary, then knead it briefly: A couple of minutes will do. Divide the dough into 6 even-sized lumps and roll each into a rough circle. The dough should not be thicker than $\frac{1}{8}$ in thick when rolled out.

INGREDIENTS

FOR THE TOMATO SAUCE
- 1 lb ripe tomatoes
- 6 tbsp olive oil
- ½ cup onions, diced into ½ in pieces
- 3 garlic cloves, left whole
- 3 basil leaves
- 1 bay leaf
- pinch of sugar
- 1 tsp sundried tomato paste
- dash of Tabasco
- salt and freshly ground black pepper

METHOD

Blanch the tomatoes in salted boiling water for 1 minute, until the skins begin to split. Remove from the water and let cool. Then remove the skins and scrape away the seeds with a teaspoon. Chop the sweet and colorful flesh, retaining the juices. Heat the olive oil and sweat the onion gently for 2–3 minutes until it is transparent. Add the chopped blanched tomatoes, juice and all, and the remaining ingredients. Bring to a boil for 3–4 minutes and then simmer gently for 30 minutes, stirring regularly. The garlic will go quite soft and sweet and the herbs will infuse the sauce with subtle aromas. When the sauce is well reduced (to about half its original volume) remove from the heat and discard the garlic and herbs.

INGREDIENTS (FOR 6 PIZZA BASES)

TOPPING 1

- tomato sauce (see opposite)
- 2 red bell peppers, thinly sliced
- 1 yellow bell pepper, thinly sliced
- 1 medium eggplant, thinly sliced
- 3 medium zucchini, thinly sliced

- 6 garlic cloves
- ¾ cup black olives
- 3 small goats' cheeses
- ½ cup olive oil
- small bunch fresh basil

METHOD

Preheat the oven to 400°F.

Prick each of the pizza bases with a fork and brush generously with tomato sauce. Arrange some of each of the vegetables, the unpeeled garlic cloves and the olives, on top of each pizza, as well as half a goat's cheese—as it is or cut into thick slices. Drizzle olive oil lightly over everything, tucking in the basil leaves under the more robust vegetables. Place on a lightly floured baking tray and bake for 15 minutes until the pizza base is crisp and lightly browned around the edges.

INGREDIENTS (FOR 6 PIZZA BASES)

TOPPING 2

- ½ cup canned artichoke hearts
- ½ cup olive oil
- 2 garlic cloves, crushed
- dash of Tabasco
- 1 lb baby spinach
- pinch of nutmeg

- 2 medium red onions
- 1½ cups feta cheese
- tomato sauce (see opposite)
- 6 sundried tomatoes in oil, sliced
- 1 heaping tbsp pine nuts
- salt and freshly ground black pepper

METHOD

Preheat the oven to 400°F.

Drain the artichoke hearts and marinate them in most of the olive oil for an hour or so, adding a little of the crushed garlic and a dash of Tabasco. Set aside. Meanwhile, sweat the spinach in 1 tbsp olive oil, with the nutmeg, remaining garlic, a pinch of salt, and some freshly ground black pepper for 1 minute. Set aside. Cut each red onion into 6 or more wedges. Break the feta into rough pieces. Prick each of the pizza bases with a fork and brush with tomato sauce. Heap on the prepared vegetables and sundried tomatoes in a generous pile, hiding most of the spinach under the artichokes and red onion. Sprinkle with the feta and pine nuts. Trickle a little olive oil on top and bake for 15–20 minutes until the edges are golden and crisp.

INGREDIENTS (FOR 6 PIZZA BASES)

TOPPING 3

- 2 medium fennel bulbs
- ½ cup olive oil
- 2 garlic cloves, crushed
- dash of Tabasco
- 2 whole mozzarella cheeses

- I head radicchio
- 3 red onions
- tomato sauce (see page 72)
- I cup freshly shredded Parmesan cheese
- salt and freshly ground black pepper

METHOD

Trim the fennel, removing any tough and fibrous ends. Cut into 8 lengthwise slices and baste generously with most of the olive oil, a bit of crushed garlic, a dash of Tabasco, salt, and pepper. Then slice the mozzarella, add to the fennel, and mix well. Set aside for an hour or more.

Preheat the oven to 400°F. Roughly chop the radicchio and cut the red onion into chunks. Prick each of the pizza bases with a fork and spread over the tomato sauce. Cover first with the radicchio, and lightly season with salt and pepper. Then top with the remaining crushed garlic, the fennel pieces, the red onion, and finally the mozzarella. Drizzle with olive oil and place in the preheated oven for 15–20 minutes until the pizza edges are crisp and golden, the mozzarella melted. and the red onion and fennel charred and softened.

GREEN BEANS WITH RED ONION CONFIT, CANNELLINI BEANS, AND TOMATOES

What might be a very typical Mediterranean combination turns Oriental with the addition of teriyaki sauce and ginger. As with most sautéed vegetables, this is delicious with rice: Try a robust combination of Italian short-grain, wild rice and Camargue red rice, generously infused with lime and cilantro and very finely diced fiery red chili pepper.

SERVES
4 − 6

INGREDIENTS

- 2 lb green beans
- ½ lb firm red tomatoes, quartered
- I cup cooked or canned cannellini beans
- 5 tbsp teriyaki sauce
- I small piece fresh chili pepper, diced
- I large handful cilantro, chopped, some leaves reserved for garnish
- I tbsp sesame seeds
- salt

FOR THE RED ONION CONFIT

- ½ lb red onions
- 6 tbsp chili pepper oil
- ½ tsp soft brown sugar
- I piece ginger, about I in long, shredded
- 2 garlic cloves, crushed
- dash of Tabasco
- salt and freshly ground black pepper

METHOD

Clean the green beans and blanch in a large pan of salted boiling water for 2–3 minutes, until *al dente*. Immediately refresh under very cold water and set aside.

For the confit, cut the red onions in half along the length, then cut into thin slices, again following the length. Heat half the chili pepper oil and sauté the onions over a gentle heat until soft, gradually adding the sugar, shredded ginger, garlic, Tabasco, salt, and pepper. The onion will caramelize and you may need to add a drop of water to dislodge any juices that stick to the pan. Transfer to a plate and set aside.

In the same pan, heat the remaining oil, and quickly sauté the green beans, adding the tomato quarters for literally 1 minute, turning and tossing the pan in large and dramatic movements (or stir vigorously). Then add the cannellini beans, teriyaki sauce, diced chili pepper, and cilantro. Place on a warmed serving plate and top with the onion confit. Garnish with more fresh cilantro and the sesame seeds.

COUSCOUS
WITH ROASTED VEGETABLES

Couscous is durum wheat and water mixed together and then rolled together to form thousands of tiny balls. It is not, as many people think, a separate kind of grain. Traditionally it is steamed in a couscousier, but this can take as long as 1½ hours. This quick method yields surprisingly good results. If you wish, serve with a bowl of yogurt seasoned with garlic, cilantro, and mint.

SERVES

6

INGREDIENTS

- 3½ cups couscous
- 3 cups boiling water
- ½ tsp bouillon powder
- 1 tbsp olive oil
- 1 onion, finely diced
- 1 heaping tsp mustard seeds
- 1 garlic clove, crushed
- salt and freshly ground black pepper

FOR THE VEGETABLES

- 1 red bell pepper, seeds and pith removed, and cut into 6
- 1 yellow bell pepper, seeds and pith removed, and cut into 6
- 1 fennel bulb, trimmed and cut into 6
- 2 medium zucchini, cut into 2 in chunks on the diagonal
- 3 red onions, cut into 6 wedges
- 2 medium eggplant, cut into 2 in chunks
- 4 tbsp olive oil
- dash of Tabasco
- 1 tbsp balsamic vinegar
- 1 garlic clove, crushed
- salt and freshly ground black pepper

METHOD

Preheat the oven to its highest setting.

Place the couscous in a large pan and pour over the boiling water and bouillon powder. The couscous will be soft as soon as the water has been absorbed.

Meanwhile, heat the olive oil and sauté the onion until golden brown, adding the mustard seeds, crushed garlic, and salt and pepper. Mix with the couscous and set aside.

For the roasted vegetables, mix all the vegetables with the olive oil, Tabasco, balsamic vinegar, garlic, and salt and pepper, and place in an ovenproof dish. Bake in the preheated oven for 35 minutes or until charred and tender. Serve piled on the couscous.

MASHED POTATO
WITH SAUTEED VEGETABLES

Mashed potatoes as a main course? Why not, especially if they are combined with such elegant partners. The type of mushroom used in the sauce will have a great impact on the final dish and I prefer morels, which are more readily available than in the past. To be sure, cultivated morels do not have the exquisite intensity of wild ones but I would rather have them than none at all.

SERVES
6 – 8

INGREDIENTS

FOR THE MASHED POTATOES
- 4 large potatoes
- ½ cup unsalted butter
- salt and white pepper

FOR THE VEGETABLES
- ½ lb baby carrots
- ½ lb asparagus
- 1 lb baby leeks, trimmed and cut on the diagonal
- ½ lb fava beans, fresh or frozen, shelled

FOR THE SAUCE
- ½ cup butter
- 2 garlic cloves, crushed
- ½ cup mushrooms (button, chestnut, chanterelles, or morels), thinly sliced
- handful of fresh sorrel, shredded
- handful of fresh chervil
- small bunch chives, finely snipped
- salt and freshly ground black pepper

METHOD

Peel the potatoes and place in a large pan of salted water. Bring to a boil and simmer until tender. Drain and mash with a potato masher and then push through a fine strainer.

If using straightaway, beat in all the butter and adjust seasoning. If not, then beat in 6 tbsp of the butter and refrigerate. To serve, warm the mashed potato in a saucepan, adding the remaining butter.

Separately blanch the carrots, asparagus, leeks, and fava beans in plenty of salted boiling water. The vegetables will need 1 minute each, the fava beans 3–4 minutes.

For the sauce, melt the butter and sauté the garlic and mushrooms for 3–4 minutes, adding salt and pepper. Add the blanched vegetables, some of the shredded sorrel, a few sprigs of chervil, and half the chives, and stir gently so that all the vegetables are coated in the butter. Very gently fold in the fava beans.

Pile the vegetables on top of the mashed potato and garnish with the remaining fresh herbs and with any remaining butter poured over.

CHICKPEA FRITTERS

AND TIKKA SAUCE

These fritters are delicious and the home-made tikka sauce is very simple to make and well worth the effort. Serve with a sautéed green vegetable.

INGREDIENTS

FOR THE FRITTERS

- I cup dried chickpeas, soaked overnight in water
- 2 cups cooked chickpeas
- 2 tbsp tikka paste
- I large red onion, diced
- juice of I lime
- I handful fresh cilantro, chopped
- ½ cup light olive oil or corn oil, for sautéing
- salt and freshly ground black pepper

FOR THE TIKKA SAUCE

- I heaping tsp ground ginger
- I heaping tsp ground coriander
- I heaping tsp cumin
- I heaping tsp turmeric
- 3 heaping tbsp very red paprika
- ½ tsp very red dried chili pepper powder
- 6 tbsp water
- 4 tbsp corn oil
- 2–3 garlic cloves, crushed to a smooth paste
- I heaping tsp tamarind paste
- ½ large chili pepper, chopped or blended very finely to form a paste
- I handful fresh cilantro, chopped
- ½ cup yogurt

METHOD

To make the fritters, place the raw soaked chickpeas in a food processor and pulverize for 15 seconds until broken down but still gritty in consistency. Mash the cooked chickpeas with a fork or potato masher until almost smooth but with just a few chickpeas nearly whole. Mix with the ground raw chickpeas. Add the tikka paste, red onion, lime juice, fresh cilantro, and salt and pepper, if required. Mix well and set aside, covered with plastic wrap, for 20 minutes for the flavors to develop.

To make the tikka sauce, mix all the spices together and add the water and then the oil. Mix thoroughly. Add the garlic, tamarind, chili pepper paste, and cilantro. Mix well and set aside in a covered bowl or jar with a lid. Add the yogurt just before serving.

Work the fritter mixture with your fingers for a few seconds to make sure it holds together properly, and form into rough patties about 3 inches in diameter and ½ in thick. Heat the oil and sauté gently for a couple of minutes on each side until golden brown and crisp. Drain on paper towels, then serve hot with the tikka sauce.

VERMOUTH MUSHROOMS ON TOASTED BRIOCHE
SERVED WITH POACHED EGG

This is a sophisticated dinner party dish to attempt when you are confident about poaching eggs. The trick is to add some clear vinegar to the water and to stir furiously around the egg as soon as you drop it in to keep all the white together. The other trick is to use a simple egg poacher and be done!

INGREDIENTS

- 6 tbsp butter
- 2 garlic cloves, finely chopped
- 2½ lb mixed mushrooms, to include dried (soaked and drained), wild, and button
- dash of tamari
- dash of Tabasco
- 4 tbsp vermouth
- 5 tbsp heavy cream
- 6 slices home-made brioche (see page 247)
- 1 tbsp clear vinegar
- 6 eggs, medium sized
- ½ lb fresh baby spinach
- salt and freshly ground black pepper

METHOD

Melt the butter in a sautéing pan and sauté the garlic over low heat for a few minutes, making sure it does not burn. Add the mushrooms, tamari, Tabasco, and salt and pepper, and sauté for a further 3–4 minutes until they are tender and release their liquor. Add the vermouth and reduce to about half, then add the cream, and stir. Remove from the heat and set aside.

Toast the slices of brioche under a broiler until they are golden brown. Remove and cover with a cloth to keep warm.

Bring a pan of salted water to a boil, add the vinegar, and carefully break in one egg. Stir all the time with a fork and, as soon as the yolk is set to your liking, remove the egg to a plate, using a slotted spoon. Repeat with the other eggs.

Gently reheat the mushrooms and stir in the spinach until it just wilts. Immediately remove from the heat.

Serve a slice of toasted brioche topped with a poached egg and surrounded with the mushrooms and spinach, with sauce spooned all around.

CANNELLONI

There is no comparison between cannelloni made with dried pasta tubes and those you make yourself with fresh lasagne sheets. There is no need to blanch the spinach. It can simply wilt in the heat.

SERVES

4 – 6

12 ROLLS

INGREDIENTS

- ¾ lb fresh spinach, washed
- scraping of fresh nutmeg
- 1 tsp olive oil
- ½ small red onion, diced
- 1 cup chestnut mushrooms, sliced
- 2 garlic cloves, crushed
- 1 tsp tamari
- 1 cup ricotta

- ¼ cup Parmesan cheese, freshly shredded
- ½ lb fresh spinach pasta sheets, cut into 3 strips, each 3½ in wide and 16 in long
- thick tomato sauce (see page 100)
- 1 cup smetana or crème fraîche
- 1 cup mascarpone cheese
- 1 cup Cheddar cheese, shredded
- salt and freshly ground black pepper

METHOD

Preheat the oven to 400°F.

Place the spinach and a little salt and pepper in a pan set over low heat for 1 minute until wilted. Drain thoroughly and add a little grated nutmeg. Chop roughly and set aside to cool.

Heat the olive oil, and when it is very hot, add first the onion and sauté for 5–6 minutes, then add the sliced mushrooms, crushed garlic, and tamari. Sauté for 1–2 minutes until browned. Mix with the spinach and set aside to cool. Then mix with the ricotta and Parmesan.

To assemble the cannelloni, lay a strip of pasta on a dry chopping board, and place a heaping tablespoon of the filling at one end of the strip. Bring the outer end over and roll to make a tube with very little overlap. Trim the ends with a sharp knife and proceed in this way until all the pasta sheets and filling are used up.

Place half the tomato sauce in an ovenproof dish and arrange the cannelloni on top, side by side in two lines. Cover with the remaining tomato sauce and then with the smetana or crème fraîche and mascarpone. Finally add the shredded Cheddar and bake in the preheated oven for 25–30 minutes until golden brown.

FILLED EGGPLANT ROLLS

Slices of potatoes, red onion, and tomatoes (see page 63) laid out on a plate in a circle make an attractive backdrop for these eggplant rolls, drizzled with a little olive oil and pesto. The smoked fontina cheese and the rich nature of eggplant make this a deeply flavored dish.

SERVES

6

INGREDIENTS

- 3 medium eggplant, cut in half lenthwise and flesh scooped out to within ¼ in of the skin
- ¾ cup olive oil
- dash of Tabasco
- 1 lb tomatoes, blanched, peeled, deseeded, and chopped
- 3 garlic cloves, crushed
- 1 tbsp balsamic vinegar
- ½ cup water
- ½ small fennel bulb, chopped
- 2 large zucchini, diced
- 2 cups canned kidney beans, including half their liquid
- ¼ cup pesto
- ½ cup smoked fontina cheese, very finely sliced
- several basil leaves, for garnish
- salt and freshly ground black pepper

METHOD

Preheat the oven to 425°F.

Brush the scooped out eggplant halves with a little olive oil, salt, pepper, and Tabasco. Bake in the preheated oven for about 40 minutes until the remaining flesh is completely soft.

Meanwhile, chop the eggplant flesh and sauté in half the remaining olive oil, with the chopped tomatoes, which will release liquid into the pan, plus the crushed garlic and the balsamic vinegar. Stir often and add the water, a little at a time, as the eggplant sticks to the pan. The eggplant will be soft in about 30 minutes. Remove from the pan and set aside.

Add the chopped fennel to the same still hot pan, adding only a touch of oil and water if you need to. A minute later, add the zucchini and sauté for a further minute or two. Finally, return the fried eggplant to the pan and mix well, adding the canned kidney beans and liquid.

Lightly baste the eggplant halves with pesto and line each with a thin slice of smoked fontina cheese. Then fill with the vegetable mixture and roll. The two ends will meet in the middle and need to be secured with 3 toothpicks. Brush with the rest of the pesto. Pour the remaining olive oil into an ovenproof dish and pack the eggplant rolls tightly together. Bake for 15 minutes, until the pesto crisps up a little. Serve hot, garnished with the basil.

CHEESE AND ONION BREAD PUDDING

This is as down-to-earth and filling as it sounds, and the kind of dish everyone secretly loves. You can make it more sophisticated by replacing the Cheddar with a smoked fontina cheese and replacing up to half the milk with heavy cream. You could also wilt some baby spinach or arugula into the egg mixture. Other vegetables such as sautéed zucchini and mushrooms are equally successful. But here is the recipe in its basic form so you can ring the changes for yourself.

SERVES
6

INGREDIENTS

- 2 tbsp unsalted butter plus 1 tbsp to butter the dish
- 3 large onions, finely sliced
- 1 tsp fresh thyme leaves
- 2 garlic cloves, finely crushed (optional)
- ½ cup freshly shredded Parmesan cheese

- 1½ cups shredded Cheddar cheese
- 1 tbsp fresh chives, finely snipped
- 8 slices wholewheat bread, crusts removed
- 3 eggs, medium sized
- 2 cups milk
- salt and freshly ground black pepper

METHOD

Preheat the oven to 375°F.

Heat the butter in a sautéing pan and sauté the onion for 10–15 minutes until soft and golden brown. Add the fresh thyme and the garlic, if using, and season with salt and pepper. Combine the Parmesan with the Cheddar and finely snipped chives, then mix with the fried onion.

Place half the bread slices in a buttered ovenproof dish, trimming the slices if necessary so that they fit snugly. Cover with half the cheese and onion mixture. Repeat with the remaining bread and finish with the rest of the cheese mixture.

Place the eggs and milk in a bowl and whisk. Season with salt and pepper, taking into account the saltiness of the cheese. Pour over the bread and cheese and place in the preheated oven for 30–35 minutes until the custard is set but still moist, and golden brown. Serve straight from the oven.

VEGETABLE BROCHETTES
WITH SPICED RICE

Almost any kind of vegetable can be skewered onto wooden or metal sticks, marinated in any manner of seasoning, and left to roast over hot coals or under ordinary broilers. Even a vegetable as hard as pumpkin can feature on a brochette, as can papaya and mango, pattypan, Belgian endive, and fennel, to name but a few. Experiment to your heart's content. You may wish to offer a variety of brochettes at the same time, keeping the longer-cooking vegetables on one stick and the faster cooking ones on another. But even mixing them is wonderful, with some vegetables completely soft and others still firm. Make cuts into the flesh of tougher vegetables to help them absorb the spices and herbs of the marinade. Dip a pastry brush lusciously into the sauce and spread generously over each vegetable, or place in a large bowl with the sauce poured on top. The mélange suggested in this recipe is daring, the striking color and sweetness of some marrying with the bitterness of others.

SERVES
6 – 8

INGREDIENTS

- 8 baby eggplant
- 8 baby zucchini
- I lb small pumpkin, unpeeled
- I papaya
- I red bell pepper
- 16 thick asparagus spears
- 4 heads Belgian endive
- 8 shallots
- 8 tomatoes
- 16 yellow and green pattypans
- I cup shiitake mushrooms
- I cup oyster mushrooms

FOR THE MARINADE

- ¾ cup olive oil
- 5 tbsp tamari
- I tbsp Tabasco
- I tbsp grain mustard
- I heaping tsp cumin
- I tbsp paprika
- juice of I½ limes
- 2 garlic cloves, crushed
- I red chili pepper, finely chopped

FOR THE RICE
- 2 cups Italian short-grain brown rice
- 1 quart water
- salt
- 2 red bell peppers
- ½ lb zucchini

- 1 large carrot
- 1 fine leek
- 1 corn on the cob
- 1 heaping tbsp finely chopped parsley
- 1 heaping tbsp finely chopped cilantro
- several sprigs very fresh cilantro, to garnish

METHOD

Mix all the marinade ingredients together and allow the flavors to mingle for as long as you can: A good hour is ideal.

Meanwhile, prepare the vegetables. Leave all the baby vegetables whole: You do not even need to remove the stalks. Cut the pumpkin and papaya into slices about 1 in wide and 4 in long. Leave the skin on both. Cut the red bell pepper into 6 large strips. Choose fat, juicy asparagus spears, trimmed to about 5 in long. Remove any brown leaves from the Belgian endive and cut into quarters. Blanch the shallots in boiling water for 1 minute and then peel. Wash the tomatoes, but leave whole. Make shallow incisions into all vegetables except the tomatoes and mushrooms.

Place all the brochette vegetables in a shallow dish and pour over half the marinade. Mix well, cover, and let marinate for at least one hour or overnight.

Place the rice in a pressure cooker with the lightly salted water. Bring to pressure, then reduce heat and cook for 15 minutes. Remove from the heat but do not remove lid for a further 5 minutes.

Meanwhile, prepare the vegetables for the rice. Remove all seeds and pith from the bell peppers and slice into the thinnest and longest possible slivers, not unlike noodles. Repeat with the zucchini, carrot, and leek. Slice the corn kernels off the sides of the cob. Then heat the reserved marinade in a wok or large pan. First add the carrots, then seconds later the leek, then the corn and finally the bell pepper and zucchini. Sauté on a high heat for a minute, taking care not to burn either the marinade or vegetables and retaining the redness of the paprika throughout. Remove half the vegetables and set aside. Immediately add the rice to those vegetables left in the pan and continue to sauté for 2 minutes, stirring all the time until the rice is hot. Remove from heat and immediately add the chopped parsley and cilantro. Taste and add more salt, Tabasco, and lime juice if you wish. Set aside and keep warm.

Preheat the broiler. Skewer the vegetables onto large sticks: Metal ones are best and won't burn under the intense heat. Brush with the marinade and place under the hot broiler for about 15 minutes, turning over at least once and removing only when all the vegetables are charred and sizzling on all sides.

Heap the rice onto a large plate and stack the brochettes on top, scattering generously with the remaining vegetable slivers and cilantro.

NOODLES WITH SAUTEED EGGPLANT AND SMOKED BEAN CURD

This recipe again combines Oriental and Mediterranean influences. It is aromatic and a good base for some of the vegetable dishes, such as broiled shiitake mushrooms with scallions (see page 166) and is perfect followed by a baked fruit dessert.

(see page 166)

SERVES

6

INGREDIENTS

- 6 tbsp olive oil mixed with 1 tbsp sesame oil (optional)
- 2 large eggplant, cut into $\frac{1}{4}$ in slices, then into thin strips
- 3 tbsp balsamic vinegar
- 3 garlic cloves, crushed
- 4 tbsp sesame seeds
- 1 piece fresh chili pepper, very finely chopped, a little reserved for garnish

- 3 tbsp cilantro, roughly chopped, half reserved for garnish
- 5 oz smoked bean curd, cut into thin strips
- 1 tbsp tamari
- dash of Tabasco
- 1 lb thick egg noodles
- $\frac{1}{4}$ cup chives, finely snipped, for garnish
- salt and freshly ground black pepper

METHOD

Heat three-quarters of the oil in a pan and, over high heat, sauté the strips of eggplant with the balsamic vinegar and the crushed garlic for 5–6 minutes until they shrivel and shrink, become golden brown, but still retain a slightly chewy texture. If they dry and stick to the pan, simply add a little water to loosen the juices from the bottom of the pan and continue sautéing until evaporated. Add 1 tbsp sesame seeds and continue to sauté for a few minutes until they begin to split and pop and generally jump about. Then add the chili pepper and cilantro and remove from heat. Set aside. In the same pan, heat the remaining oil and sauté the bean curd strips with the tamari, and Tabasco. Again, toss and turn until the bean curd goes brown and begins to crisp in places, also adding 1 tbsp sesame seeds and sautéing as before.

Meanwhile, bring a large pan of salted water to a boil and cook the noodles for 4 minutes or according to packet instructions. Drain and mix with the eggplant and bean curd. Arrange individual servings by twisting the noodles around a fork and heaping onto the plates, and garnish with the remaining sesame seeds, chili pepper, chives, and cilantro.

POLENTA GNOCCHI
WITH BROWNED VEGETABLES

This is my favorite way of eating polenta. At Cranks, we serve the polenta in triangular pieces, laid out on a large and colorful dish laden with all kinds of browned or broiled vegetables.

INGREDIENTS

- 1 quart milk or water
- ¾ cup butter
- 2½ cups polenta
- 3 egg yolks
- 1 cup Parmesan cheese, freshly shredded
- pinch of nutmeg (optional)
- 2 tbsp basil, finely shredded
- salt and freshly ground black pepper

FOR THE VEGETABLES

- 2 fennel bulbs, cut lengthwise into 6
- 1 red bell pepper, cut into 6 long strips
- 1 yellow bell pepper, cut into 6 long strips
- 3 small red onions, cut into quarters
- 1 large eggplant, cut into 2 in chunks
- 3 medium zucchini, cut on the slant into thick slices
- 2 garlic bulbs, cloves separated but left unpeeled
- ½ cup olive oil
- dash of Tabasco
- 6 tomatoes
- salt and freshly ground black pepper

METHOD

For the gnocchi, heat the milk or water with a pinch of salt and a pat of the butter. When it boils, pour in the polenta in a continuous stream, and stir vigorously to avoid lumps forming. Simmer gently for 15–20 minutes, stirring regularly.

Remove from heat and add the egg yolks, half the Parmesan, and the nutmeg if using. Pour the mixture onto a smooth board or work surface that has been slightly dampened. Smooth the mixture down so it is of equal thickness all over. Let cool, then cut out circles 2 inches in diameter with a pastry cutter.

Preheat the oven to 400°F. Butter an ovenproof dish and arrange the gnocchi in it so that they slightly overlap. Melt the remaining butter, pour over the gnocchi, and place in the oven for 20–25 minutes until golden brown. Remove from oven and sprinkle with the remaining Parmesan and basil.

For the vegetables, preheat the oven to its highest setting. Place all the vegetables except the tomatoes in a dish with most of the oil, a little Tabasco, and salt and pepper. Place in the oven and bake for 35–40 minutes until all the vegetables are charred and slightly shrivelled. Add the tomatoes about halfway through the cooking time, making sure that they are basted in olive oil. Place the polenta on a serving platter and pile the vegetables on top. Serve at once.

FILLED BAKED POTATOES

Here is a simple, warming meal in the hand, with an infinite possibility of fillings, which you can make as grand or simple as you like. Simply oil the skins first to avoid their otherwise rather awful dullness. Or use smaller potatoes and make more than one filling at a time so you can enjoy them all at one sitting.

SERVES

6

INGREDIENTS

- 6 large baking potatoes
- corn oil

FILLING 1

- 1 cup button mushrooms, thickly sliced
- 1 tbsp olive oil
- dash of Tabasco
- 1 tbsp tamari
- 1 egg, medium sized, beaten
- 1 tbsp butter
- 1½ cups Cheddar cheese, shredded
- ½ cup sour cream

- 2 tsp grain mustard
- 2 tsp snipped chives
- 1 garlic clove, crushed
- salt and freshly ground black pepper

FILLING 2

- 1 egg, medium sized, beaten
- ½ cup black olives, roughly chopped
- 1 cup mozzarella cheese, shredded
- 1 garlic clove, crushed
- 4 sundried tomatoes in oil, cut into thin slivers
- handful of fresh basil, finely chopped
- salt and freshly ground black pepper

METHOD

Preheat the oven to 350°F. Oil the potatoes and bake for 45 minutes or until soft.

FILLING 1

Sauté the mushrooms in the olive oil and season with a dash of Tabasco, tamari, and salt and pepper. Cut the tops from the potatoes and scoop out the flesh with a spoon, leaving a shell ½ in thick. Place the potato flesh in a bowl and mix with the mushrooms, beaten egg, butter, shredded cheese, sour cream, mustard, chives, crushed garlic, and salt and pepper. Scoop this back into the potatoes and bake at 350°F for 10–15 minutes.

FILLING 2

Proceed as above, mixing the potato flesh with the egg, olives, mozzarella, crushed garlic, sundried tomatoes, basil, salt, and pepper. Bake as before.

WILD MUSHROOM FRICASSEE

There are now so many different varieties of mushrooms available at supermarkets and specialist suppliers that there is barely an excuse to settle for the tasteless polystyrene lookalikes. Oyster mushrooms, which have taken better than most to cultivation, are a tame equivalent of their originals, if you are to judge by their size. On the Suffolk coast, I have picked them 12 inches in diameter, cleaned and cooked them in nothing more than butter, garlic, white wine, and salt and pepper. Delicious.

Use as many varieties as you can and always supplement with mixed dried mushrooms, which often contain some pieces of the rare and astronomically expensive morels. Dried mushrooms have the depth of flavor required for a dish like this one. Adding a touch of tamari and brandy to the hot soaking water brings out the flavor. Also take great care in cleaning fresh mushrooms, especially chanterelles, and in ridding them of their grit by wiping gently with paper towels or using a small soft brush. Do not wash them in water. Serve this with the Individual Soufflés on page 93 for an extravagant meal.

SERVES
6

INGREDIENTS

- 1¼ cups dried assorted wild mushrooms
- 2 cups hot water
- 1 tbsp tamari
- 1 tbsp brandy
- 2 garlic cloves, crushed
- ½ tsp grain mustard
- 3 tbsp butter
- ¼ tsp soft brown sugar
- 2 large sprigs fresh tarragon

- 1 cup shiitake mushrooms, tough stalks removed, cut into thick slivers
- 1¼ cups oyster mushrooms
- 1¼ cups chanterelles, carefully cleaned
- 2 scallions, finely sliced
- ½ lb baby spinach
- 1 tbsp heavy cream
- salt and freshly ground black pepper

METHOD

Soak the dried mushrooms in the hot water together with the tamari and brandy. Strain through a strainer lined with cheesecloth, holding the strainer over a bowl so as to catch all the liquid. Put the mushrooms and strained soaking liquid in a large sautéing pan and bring to a boil together with the crushed garlic, mustard, and butter, stirring continuously. Then add the sugar which simply rounds off the taste. Add the whole sprigs of tarragon and continue to stir occasionally as the juices reduce to about half their original volume.

Add the shiitake mushrooms and simmer for a couple of minutes, then carefully fold in the oyster mushrooms and cook for just 1 minute. Then, again very carefully, add the chanterelles. Remove the wilted sprigs of tarragon. One minute later add the scallion and the baby spinach cooking until it just wilts. Remove from heat and stir in the heavy cream and season to taste. The fricassée is brilliant with pasta, simply served on toast, or as a luxurious filling for fluffy omelets.

INDIVIDUAL SOUFFLES

These are based on Delia Smith's twice-baked soufflés, but I have replaced the Cheddar with Gruyère and the grain mustard with chopped sorrel, but you could use both. I've also added a whole garlic clove to infuse the milk along with the onion. If sorrel is unavailable, you could try spinach or arugula. Serve with the Mushroom Fricassée on page 91.

SERVES
4

INGREDIENTS

- 2 cups milk
- 1 large onion, halved
- 1 garlic clove, left whole
- 6–7 whole peppercorns
- ¼ cup unsalted butter
- ½ cup self-rising flour

- 4 eggs, medium sized, separated
- 1–2 sorrel leaves, finely chopped
- pinch of freshly ground nutmeg
- 2 cups Gruyère cheese, shredded
- salt

METHOD

Butter 4 x 6 fl oz ramekins. Preheat the oven to 350°F.

Bring the milk to simmering point with the halved onion, peeled garlic clove, the peppercorns, and a little salt. Cover and let sit for 30 minutes to infuse the flavours. Strain.

Make a roux by melting the butter and adding the flour, stirring all the time until both are well amalgamated and leave the sides of the pan clean. Gradually add the warmed milk, stirring the whole time, and cook gently for 2 minutes. Transfer to mixing bowl and cool slightly.

Meanwhile, whisk the egg whites until stiff and set aside. Beat the egg yolks, sorrel, and nutmeg into the cooled sauce. Fold in three-quarters of the cheese then the whisked egg whites. Pour into the prepared ramekins.

Place the ramekins in a shallow ovenproof dish and fill with hot water reaching halfway up the sides of the ramekins. Bake for 15 minutes, then remove from the oven and set aside. At this point, the soufflés can be left for several hours.

For the second baking, transfer the soufflés to a baking sheet, sprinkle with the remaining cheese, and bake at 400°F for 20 minutes. Serve immediately.

FILLED GIANT PUMPKIN
WITH HERBED WHIPPED CREAM

If ever there was a convivial main course to serve among friends, this is it. I have made Raymond Blanc's version in which he serves pumpkin soup in its own shell, loved the ingenuity of it, and wanted for a long time to come up with a version of my own. This is it.

INGREDIENTS

- I pumpkin, approximately 3 lb, top reserved and seeds removed
- 4 tbsp olive oil
- I tbsp tamari
- I tbsp red wine or brandy
- dash of Tabasco
- I garlic clove, crushed

FOR THE HERBED WHIPPED CREAM

- 2 cups heavy cream
- I bunch cilantro, finely chopped
- juice of ½ lime
- I garlic clove, crushed
- I small piece chili pepper, very finely chopped
- salt and freshly ground black pepper

FOR THE FILLING

- 4 medium carrots, cut into chunks
- 4 medium parsnips, cut into chunks
- 2 fennel bulbs, cut into wedges
- 5 tbsp olive oil
- 4 medium zucchini
- I lb baby onions
- 2 tbsp butter or extra olive oil
- I tbsp soft brown sugar
- ⅓ cup whole almonds, blanched and skins removed
- salt and freshly ground black pepper

METHOD

To make the filling, preheat the oven to its highest setting. Place the carrots, parsnips, and fennel on a baking tray and baste with most of the olive oil. Baste the zucchini with the remaining oil and place in a separate tray. Roast the carrots, fennel, and parsnips for 30–35 minutes until well browned, but remember that they will be returned to the oven for a further 10 minutes so don't over-roast. Do the same with the zucchini, but bake for only 25 minutes. Remove from the oven and set aside.

To bake the pumpkin, lower the oven temperature to 300°F. Make 7 or 8 skin-deep slits on the outside to prevent the pumpkin from splitting during cooking. Also make a few criss-cross cuts on the inside so that the pumpkin flesh can better absorb the seasoning.

Mix the olive oil, tamari, red wine or brandy, Tabasco, and crushed garlic and brush all over the inside of the pumpkin, making sure it gets right into the flesh. Wrap the pumpkin in foil and bake in the preheated oven for 50–60 minutes until tender but not too soft. Remove the foil and increase the oven temperature to maximum for 10 minutes so the flesh can caramelize slightly.

Meanwhile, place the unpeeled baby onions in a pan of boiling water for 1 minute to loosen the skins slightly. Drain, peel, and return to the same pan with the butter and sugar. Add ¼ cup water (or enough to cover the onions) and cover with a lid. Bring to a boil, then simmer for about 25 minutes, adding more water if necessary, and cooking until the onions are soft and caramelized.

Meanwhile, make the herbed cream by lightly whipping the cream and gently folding in all the other ingredients. Set aside.

Return the roasted vegetables to the oven to heat through while the pumpkin is undergoing its final 10 minutes' cooking. Mix the carrots, parsnips, fennel, and zucchini together with the glazed onions and almonds, season to taste, and fill the pumpkin with the mixture. Serve with the herbed cream sauce on the side.

NOTE

A quicker filling can be made by simply blanching the carrots and fennel for 2 minutes, adding to the glazed onions and the zucchini, and continuing to sauté for 5–6 minutes until tender and well coated in the onion juices.

MIDDLE EASTERN POTATO CASSEROLE

A dish of this simplicity depends entirely on slow cooking so that the flavors have plenty of time to develop.

SERVES

8

INGREDIENTS

- 3½ lb potatoes
- 4½ cups onions, diced
- ¼ cup olive oil
- I tsp turmeric
- I tsp ground coriander
- 2½ fl oz water
- dash of Tabasco

- 3 garlic cloves, crushed
- 4–5 saffron strands, dissolved in ¼ cup hot water
- I cup raisins
- I tbsp fresh parsley
- I tbsp fresh cilantro
- salt and freshly ground black pepper

METHOD

Peel the potatoes and cut into even-sized pieces and place in a pan of cold, salted water. Bring to a boil until tender but still firm, as they are going to cook further. Drain and set aside.

Sauté the onion in the olive oil until transparent and add the turmeric and ground coriander. Continue to sauté until the spices are well absorbed and the grittiness is all cooked out. Add the potatoes and the water. Add the salt, pepper, Tabasco, and crushed garlic, and simmer for a further 7–8 minutes. Now add the saffron stock and raisins and continue to simmer for at least another 10 minutes, until the potatoes are tender and the sauce is thickened and a rich golden color, with the flavors mingled into an evocative whiff of the Orient.

Just before serving, add the chopped parsley and cilantro and, if you wish, a further glug of olive oil, gently stirred in.

SPAGHETTI
WITH RADICCHIO

The sweet, soft flesh of freshly roasted garlic–this time wrapped in foil to preserve the sweetness and to avoid browning–adds further depth to this dish, which is as simple and elegant as a pasta can be. You could use a linguine or tagliatelle for this dish. I made it with spaghetti simply because I wanted to add a little sophistication to this most prosaic pasta. Serve with a large portion of spinach lightly sautéed and tossed in butter or olive oil with nothing but salt and freshly ground pepper for seasoning.

SERVES
6

INGREDIENTS

- 6 garlic cloves
- 2–3 heads radicchio
- 1 tbsp olive oil
- 1½ lb spaghetti
- 4 tbsp butter

- 1 tsp grain mustard
- 2 cups heavy cream
- freshly shredded Parmesan cheese, to serve
- salt and freshly ground black pepper

METHOD

Preheat the oven to 425°F. Wrap the garlic loosely in a piece of foil and bake for about 20 minutes or until soft. Let cool slightly and scoop out the flesh.

Meanwhile, separate the radicchio leaves, rinse gently, and dry in a salad spinner or between two clean dishcloths. Bunch the leaves together, chop roughly, and set aside.

Bring a large pan of salted boiling water to a boil, add the olive oil to prevent the pasta from sticking, and immediately add the pasta, holding it all as a big bunch in your hand and lowering it gently into the water as it begins to soften. Reduce the heat so that the water does not boil over, and stir the pasta a couple of times at the beginning with a fork to separate out the long strands.

Meanwhile, melt the butter in a large saucepan over low heat and add the radicchio, tossing and turning for just 1 minute so it wilts but retains as much of its color as possible. Remove from the heat.

When the pasta is *al dente*, drain, run briefly under cold water to remove the excess starch, and immediately add to the pan with the radicchio. Add the garlic flesh, the grain mustard, and the heavy cream. Season with salt and pepper and gently bring to a boil, slowly turning the pasta over all the time. Serve immediately with Parmesan.

SOUBISE RICE

This is a kind of risotto made with long-grain rice instead of Italian, short, rounded rice. Unlike classical risotto, it is not stirred during cooking, but left to absorb the wine and stock as it gently simmers. I've added fennel to the onion for an even sweeter, more delicate flavor and, if you wish, add sautéed mushrooms or spinach toward the end of the cooking time.

You could also serve it straight from the pan, simply garnished with fresh herbs, rather than bake it with bread crumbs, but this does give it a homely feel which makes it perfect for family meals.

SERVES
4 – 6

INGREDIENTS

- 5 tbsp butter
- 2 cups onions, diced
- 2 garlic cloves, finely chopped (optional)
- 1 fennel bulb, chopped into ½ in dice
- 2 cups Basmati rice
- ¾ cup dry white wine
- 1½ cups hot light vegetable stock

- 1 bay leaf
- ¾ cup freshly shredded Parmesan cheese
- ¼ cup heavy cream
- 2½ cups fresh soft white bread crumbs
- 1 bunch fresh chives, snipped very small
- salt and freshly ground black pepper

METHOD

Melt the butter in a pan and cook the onion and garlic gently, with the lid on, for about 30 minutes, adding the fennel about halfway through, until tender but not browned.

Add the rice and stir for 10 minutes. Pour in the wine and hot stock together with salt and the bay leaf. Bring to a simmer, stir, and then cover the pan and cook for 15–20 minutes until the liquid is absorbed and the rice is tender. Remove the bay leaf and stir in the Parmesan and heavy cream.

Preheat the oven to 400°F. Lightly butter an ovenproof dish and fill with the rice mixture. Sprinkle the bread crumbs mixed with the chives over the rice and bake in the preheated oven for 15 minutes until the bread crumbs are a pale golden color. Serve with a green salad and steamed broccoli tossed in olive oil and grain mustard.

LASAGNE

Poor old lasagne: What a part of the culinary institution, yet how maligned and how derided it has become. Lasagne appears in its various guises in vegetarian as well as non-vegetarian restaurants throughout the land. Every supermarket chilled and frozen cabinet boasts at least one example. It has become almost a joke dish, the last refuge for soggy pasta and overcooked vegetables floating in watery and undercooked sauces. But here is an example of lasagne with all its many layers of colors, still warming and rich, but light and modern too.

INGREDIENTS

- 10–12 sheets fresh lasagne, preferably spinach
- ¾ cup sour cream or light cream
- 2 cups smoked fontina cheese or another hard cheese such as Cheddar or Gruyère

TOMATO SAUCE
- 1 fl oz olive oil
- 1 medium onion, diced
- 2 cups cannned whole, peeled tomatoes
- 2 garlic cloves, finely sliced
- 1 large handful basil, some whole leaves reserved
- salt and freshly ground black pepper

FILLING 1
- 3 cups petit pois
- 4 tbsp butter
- 1 lb fennel, trimmed and cut into 1 in chunks
- 1 garlic clove, finely sliced

- 1 tbsp all purpose flour
- ½ cup heavy cream
- salt and freshly ground black pepper

FILLING 2
- 1 fl oz olive oil
- 1 large eggplant, cut into 1 in chunks
- 1 garlic clove, crushed
- dash of Tabasco

FILLING 3
- 1 lb spinach, washed and stalks removed
- pinch of nutmeg
- 1 garlic clove, crushed
- 3 tbsp Greek yogurt, light cream or sour cream
- salt and freshly ground black pepper

First make the tomato sauce. Heat the oil, then add the onion and sauté until transparent, then add the canned tomatoes and crush with a wooden spoon to make smaller pieces, and the finely sliced garlic. Add the basil, salt, and pepper, and cook gently for about 25 minutes until all the excess liquid has evaporated and the sauce is thick. Remove the cooked basil and replace with some freshly chopped leaves.

In the meantime, make *Filling 1*. Blanch the petits pois in boiling salted water for 5 minutes, drain and refresh under cold water. Melt the butter in a saucepan and gently sauté the fennel and garlic until tender. Add the petits pois, mix well, and sprinkle the flour on top. Stir thoroughly until it is well absorbed, season, and then add the heavy cream to make a rich sauce for the fennel and peas. Set aside.

For *Filling 2*, heat the olive oil and sauté the eggplant pieces with the garlic and Tabasco until they are browned and tender. Set aside.

Finally, for *Filling 3*, wilt the spinach in a saucepan placed over medium heat in only the water which may be clinging to it for no more than 1 minute. Immediately strain off any excess liquid and season lightly with nutmeg, salt, and pepper, and a little crushed garlic. Add the Greek yogurt, sour cream, or light cream, and set aside.

Preheat the oven to 400°F. Place a generous layer of the tomato sauce in the bottom of an oval ovenproof dish, then a layer of pasta sheets, trimmed to fit if necessary. Then alternate layers of each of the filling mixtures, with pasta sheets in between until all fillings and pasta are used up. Finish off with a layer of tomato sauce, which will be the most liquid of all fillings and which must completely cover the pasta so that it does not dry out. Spread with the sour cream or light cream. Finally, add the shredded cheese on top and bake in the preheated oven for 25–30 minutes until the cheese is brown and melted and bubbling.

POTATO GALETTE

WITH BABY VEGETABLES IN SAFFRON, THYME, LIME, AND CHILI PEPPER BUTTER

This is most definitely sophisticated enough for a dinner party or other special occasion. Waxy potatoes, such as the French Charlotte potatoes, when cooked slowly are very different indeed from the common baking or boiling potatoes–especially here as they take on the orange hue and the pungent, earthy, even slightly bitter aroma of saffron. Spanish La Mancha saffron is by far the best and worth treating yourself to. Buy the filaments or strands rather than the powder and keep them in a cool, dark, dry place. You may wish to use only saffron in this recipe and omit the turmeric altogether.

If you cannot find purple sprouting broccoli, which has a fairly short season, you can use green broccoli or replace altogether with another green vegetable such as green beans. This dish can be served in an informal fashion, with the potatoes in one dish and the baby vegetables and chanterelles in another, but for a smarter presentation, place slices of potatoes in concentric rings on individual warmed plates and pile the vegetables in the center in a delicate mound.

INGREDIENTS

- 3 lb waxy potatoes
- ½ cup olive oil
- ½ cup water
- 2 garlic cloves, finely sliced
- handful of fresh basil leaves
- 1 tsp turmeric (optional) or replace with extra saffron
- 6–7 saffron strands
- salt and freshly ground black pepper

FOR THE VEGETABLES
- pinch of saffron strands
- ¾ lb baby carrots with their leaves left on

- ¼ lb purple sprouting broccoli
- ¼ lb fine asparagus spears
- ½ cup butter
- 2 garlic cloves, finely chopped
- dash of Tabasco
- small bunch of chives, finely snipped, or 1 tbsp fresh thyme leaves, left whole
- juice of ½ lime
- 1 small piece fresh chili pepper, very finely chopped
- 1½ cups chanterelle mushrooms
- 1 tsp tamari (optional)
- salt and freshly ground black pepper

METHOD

Preheat the oven to 400°F.

Peel the potatoes and preferably slice thinly by hand so they leak out less water, although for a very even finish you may wish to use a food processor set on a ⅛ in blade. Pat the slices dry between two clean dishcloths. Then mix with the olive oil, water, and all the seasonings. Place in an ovenproof dish covered with a lid or in a dish covered with aluminum foil. Bake in the preheated oven for 1 hour, by which time the potatoes will have softened but retained their shape and texture. They will also have turned a lovely yellow. Remove from the heat before they go brown or begin to crisp.

Meanwhile, prepare the vegetables. First, soak a good pinch of saffron filaments in a couple of tablespoons of hot water and set aside for 10–15 minutes.

Lightly scrape the skin off the carrots (this is optional), then trim the purple broccoli into thin stems with only the smallest end bits removed. Similarly, remove only the very ends from the asparagus spears.

Bring a pan of salted water to a boil and blanch each of the vegetables separately for 1 minute, quickly removing one kind from the water before adding the next. It is essential, especially with the broccoli, that you refresh the vegetables under very cold water before moving on to the next stage so they retain their color. Take care also with the carrot leaves that they wilt but don't fall apart.

Next, gently heat almost all of the butter and garlic in a large pan, reserving a little butter for the mushrooms, adding a dash of Tabasco, and most of the fresh chives or thyme leaves. Also add the reserved saffron and liquid and stir briskly with a small whisk. Finally, add the lime juice, finely chopped chili pepper, and salt and pepper to taste. Continue to whisk for a minute or so. Set aside.

When ready to serve, sauté the chanterelles in a separate pan with the remaining butter and the tamari, if using, for a minute. Add these and the rest of the vegetables to the saffron butter, turning them over gently and folding in the remaining chives or thyme at the same time.

Lay the potatoes out on the plate as described and build the baby vegetables up into a pile on top. Pour any remaining saffron and herb butter all over and serve garnished with any remaining chives.

CHICKPEA CASSEROLE
WITH SPINACH

This is one of the best-sellers at Cranks. You can make it more interesting by serving a rich Greek yogurt on the side, abundantly mixed with chopped cilantro and finely minced garlic. This and the bean casserole (see page 110) benefit from this kind of cold contrast. The casserole can be made in advance and in fact improves by being left overnight so that the flavors of the herbs and spices can develop. But in that case, only add the spinach when you have reheated the casserole the next day.

INGREDIENTS

- 2 cups chickpeas, soaked overnight or for at least 2 hours
- 2½ cups onions, diced
- ½ cup olive oil
- 2–3 garlic cloves, finely chopped
- 2 tsp ground coriander
- 2 tsp turmeric
- 1 tsp cumin
- 1 scant tsp ground bay leaf

- 1 tbsp paprika
- 1½ cups potatoes, cut into 1 in chunks
- 1½ cups carrots, cut into 1 in chunks
- 1 small piece fresh chili pepper, very finely chopped
- ½ lb fresh spinach, washed and with the stalks removed
- dash of Tabasco
- salt and freshly ground black pepper

METHOD

Cook the soaked chickpeas in a pan of simmering water for 1½–2 hours until they are tender. Do not add any salt at any point as this hinders the tenderizing process.

Meanwhile, sauté the diced onion in the olive oil until transparent. Add the garlic and all the herbs and spices and continue to sauté, adding some water just before the garlic browns. Simmer gently for 5 minutes or more or until all the water is absorbed and you are left with a thick sauce.

Add the potatoes, carrots, and chili pepper, and enough water to just cover and cover with a lid. Stir regularly, adding more water if necessary until the potatoes and carrots are just barely tender. Add the drained chickpeas and continue to cook for a further 10–15 minutes so that they can absorb all the flavors. At the last minute, stir in the spinach so that it just wilts. Add more salt and pepper and Tabasco to taste. Serve hot.

PUMPKIN AND WATERCRESS GNOCCHI
WITH GREEN AND PURPLE BASIL

These gnocchi are sunshine-colored with bright green and purple streaks. The watercress and scallion cut through the sweet, thick consistency of the pumpkin and bring a crisp, fresh element to the gnocchi. Use a brightly colored pumpkin with flesh that is neither too tough nor too watery.

INGREDIENTS

- 1½ lb pumpkin or butternut squash
- 1 cup all purpose white flour, sifted
- ⅓ cup Parmesan cheese, freshly shredded
- ½ cup watercress leaves, chopped
- 1 scallion, finely sliced, green part included
- ¼ cup small green basil leaves, some reserved for garnish
- ¼ cup small purple basil leaves
- salt and freshly ground black pepper

FOR THE SAUCE

- ¾ cup olive oil
- ½ cup watercress, large stalks removed, then roughly chopped
- ¼ cup Parmesan cheese, freshly shredded
- 1 garlic clove, very finely chopped
- salt and freshly ground black pepper

METHOD

Peel the pumpkin, cut into 1¼ in chunks and place in a heavy-bottomed saucepan, just covered with water, and seasoned with a little salt and pepper. Bring to a boil, then simmer for 10 minutes until tender. Drain well, mash with a fork or potato masher, and add the sifted flour. Mix well until thoroughly incorporated, then add the Parmesan, chopped watercress, sliced scallion, and the whole green and purple basil leaves. Add salt and pepper to taste. Shape the mixture with your fingers–lightly dipped in flour–into elongated pieces the size of walnuts and set aside.

To make the sauce, mix the oil, chopped watercress, Parmesan, garlic, and salt and pepper in a bowl and set aside.

Bring a large pan of salted water to a boil. Test one gnocchi first to make sure that it does not fall apart when cooking. If it does, add a little more flour. Drop in the gnocchi and poach for 2 minutes until cooked and no longer floury.

Place the drained gnocchi in a large flat bowl, pour the sauce all over, and serve at once, garnished with green basil leaves.

HOMITY PIE

Homity Pie has been on the menu at Cranks since its very early days and it is a favorite with many regular customers. It first appeared on the menu as individual pies, with the filling set in individual wholewheat pie shells. These were much imitated and can still be seen on deli counters in England. It was then decided that the mix, filling and warming and old-fashioned as it was, should form the whole of the dish, so out went the wholewheat dough: In perfect timing with the demise of the old wicker lampshades and the faded image of 1960s vegetarian cooking.

By a happy coincidence, it now fits perfectly into the revival of good old-fashioned British home cooking. You could easily add a layer of tomato sauce in the middle or a layer of cooked spinach, or both.

SERVES

6

INGREDIENTS

- 2 lb potatoes
- 4 tbsp butter
- 1 cup sour cream
- 1 fl oz corn oil
- 1 garlic clove, crushed

- ¾ cup petit pois
- 1 cup onion, diced
- ¾ cup mature Cheddar cheese, shredded
- salt and freshly ground black pepper

METHOD

Preheat the oven to 375°F.

Peel the potatoes and place them in a pan of cold salted water. Bring to a boil and cook for 30 minutes, until the potatoes are soft. Drain and add the butter, sour cream, oil, garlic, and seasoning. Mash thoroughly with a potato masher.

Meanwhile, bring a separate smaller pan of salted water to a boil and add the petits pois. Blanch for 3–4 minutes and drain. Add the petits pois and onions to the potato mixture. Mix well and transfer to a buttered ovenproof dish. Finally, top with the shredded cheese and bake in the preheated oven for 25–30 minutes until golden brown.

VEGETABLE PAELLA

By using an array of strongly flavored ingredients, such as black olives and sundried tomatoes, this vegetarian paëlla loses none of the intense taste of the original. It is made here with short-grain organic brown rice which adds body to the dish.

INGREDIENTS

- 2 cups short-grain organic brown rice
- 1 tbsp turmeric
- 3 heaping tbsp paprika
- 4 tbsp tamari
- 1 garlic clove, cut in half
- a few saffron strands
- 1 bay leaf
- ½ cup olive oil
- ½ cup water
- 1 lb zucchini, chopped into large dice

- 2 red bell peppers, cut into 2 in pieces
- 1 large red onion, chopped into large dice
- kernels from 2 corn on the cob
- dash of Tabasco
- 3 garlic cloves, crushed
- ½ cup sundried tomatoes in oil, cut into strips
- ¾ cup Provençal black olives, left whole
- ¼ cup parsley, finely chopped
- handful of fresh basil
- salt and freshly ground black pepper

METHOD

Place the rice in a heavy-bottomed pan and add water according to packet directions. Add a little of the turmeric and paprika to the water, as well as the tamari, the halved clove of garlic, the saffron, and the bay leaf. Cover, bring to a boil, and immediately reduce to a gentle simmer for the next 45 minutes or until there is no water left in the pan and several holes have appeared on the surface. Though this is not necessary, I rinse the rice under cold water to remove any stickiness as it has to cook again and is much better when it stays light with the grains well separated.

Meanwhile, heat three-quarters of the olive oil and add the remaining paprika and turmeric together with the water and cook on a gentle heat until no graininess can be detected in the spices. Add more water if necessary, and simmer until reduced to a thick and homogenous paste.

Heat the remaining olive oil and sauté first the zucchini for a minute or so, and then briefly the red bell peppers. Sauté the red onion separately so that it remains firm, and add the corn kernels. Sauté briefly, adding the Tabasco, crushed garlic, and season. Mix all the vegetables together and cook for 3–4 minutes, adjusting the seasoning.

Add the vegetables and the cooked spice paste to the rice. Finally, add the sundried tomatoes, black olives, and the fresh herbs. Stir well over a high heat for 2–3 minutes and invert onto a dish. Serve at once.

BLACK AND RED BEAN CASSEROLE

WITH LIME AND CILANTRO CREAM

This is a really delicious vegetarian chili and seems to be a perennial favorite. You can make it as spicy as you like and add fresh cilantro and fresh chili pepper as a garnish. Lime in the yogurt or sour cream is refreshing and delicious. The guacamole is lighter and more mousse-like than usual due to the high-speed food processing. Serve the casserole with flour or corn tortillas and shredded cheese, or tortilla chips and sour cream, or both.

INGREDIENTS

- 1 cup dried red kidney beans
- 1 cup dried black kidney beans
- ½ cup olive oil
- 1 cup onion, diced
- 3–4 garlic cloves, finely chopped
- 1 tbsp paprika
- 1 piece fresh chili pepper, finely chopped
- ½ cup carrots, chopped into ½ in cubes
- thick tomato sauce (see page 100)
- ½ cup corn, fresh off the cob or frozen
- dash of Tabasco
- 1 bunch fresh cilantro, leaves only
- salt and freshly ground black pepper

FOR THE LIME AND CILANTRO CREAM

- 1 cup sour cream or yogurt
- handful of fresh cilantro, roughly chopped
- juice of ½ lime

FOR THE GUACAMOLE

- 2 ripe avocados
- 5 tbsp water
- 2 garlic cloves, crushed
- 3 tbsp olive oil
- 2–3 ripe tomatoes, deseeded and finely chopped
- salt and freshly ground black pepper

METHOD

Soak the kidney beans overnight, then drain, and boil in plenty of water until tender. This may take 1–2 hours.

Heat the olive oil in a pan and sauté the onion until brown, adding the garlic about halfway through the cooking. Add the salt, pepper, paprika, fresh chili pepper, and the carrots, and continue to cook until they are *al dente* and the spices have turned into a thick homogenous paste. Add the drained, cooked kidney beans and then the tomato sauce, and simmer until reduced. Stir in the corn and cook for a further few minutes.

Finally, adjust the seasoning with Tabasco, salt, and pepper. Continue to simmer gently for 6–7 minutes, taking care that the mixture does not dry out and, more importantly, that the sauce and vegetables form a cohesive whole with no trace of wateriness. Remove from the heat and add the fresh cilantro.

For the lime and cilantro cream, mix the sour cream or yogurt with the second quantity of cilantro, as well as the lime juice and salt to your taste.

To make the guacamole, peel the avocados, remove the pits, cut into quarters, and place in a food processor with the water and the crushed garlic and olive oil. Blend to a smooth paste. Transfer to a bowl and add the tomatoes. Grind black peppercorns over the surface and serve at once to avoid discoloration.

PEA AND ASPARAGUS RISOTTO

WITH FAVA BEANS

Frozen fava beans, especially the baby variety, are consistently good. If time is precious, fresh young peas are available ready-podded in the summer. Frozen petits pois are a good substitute.

SERVES
6

INGREDIENTS

- 1½ quarts light vegetable stock (see page 42)
- 4 tbsp unsalted butter
- 1 tbsp olive oil
- 1 onion, very finely chopped
- 2½ cups shelled young fresh peas or frozen petit pois
- 2½ cups fava beans, fresh or frozen
- 2 garlic cloves, very finely chopped
- 1½ cups Arborio or short-grain white rice
- ½ lb asparagus
- 3 tbsp flat leaf parsley, chopped
- ¾ cup Parmesan cheese, freshly shredded
- salt and freshly ground black pepper

METHOD

Bring the stock to a boil and keep simmering gently for use throughout the cooking process.

Heat half the butter and the olive oil in a heavy-bottomed saucepan and sauté the onion until pale golden and soft. Mix in the peas and fava beans at this stage, if using fresh ones, as well as the chopped garlic. Cook over low heat for 10 minutes, adding a few spoonfuls of stock during the cooking. Add the rice and sauté for 2 minutes until it goes partly translucent. Add about half the stock to the rice. Stir well and bring back to a boil. Simmer gently, stirring occasionally, and adding the rest of the stock a little at a time, until the rice is *al dente*.

Meanwhile, bring a pan of salted water to a boil and blanch the trimmed asparagus for 1 minute. Drain.

Just before serving, add the parsley and remaining butter to the risotto. Season with salt and pepper and, at the last minute, add 5 tbsp of the Parmesan and the asparagus. Serve at once with the remaining cheese handed round separately.

NOTE

If using frozen peas and fava beans, blanch them first in plenty of salted water, refresh, and add them a few minutes before the rice is done.

EGGPLANT AND FENNEL SAUTE

This is a rich combination of vegetables enhanced by the meltingly soft consistency of the eggplant. Serve with polenta, pasta, or even potatoes and a mixed salad for a light and satisfying meal.

SERVES

6

INGREDIENTS

- ¾ cup olive oil
- 2–3 garlic cloves, crushed
- 2 fennel bulbs, cut into 1½ in chunks
- 1 lb eggplant, cut into 1½ in chunks
- dash of Tabasco

- handful of basil leaves
- 1 lb tomatoes, cut into quarters
- ¾ cup fresh Parmesan cheese, sliced into fine slivers
- salt and freshly ground black pepper

METHOD

Heat the olive oil gently and stir in the crushed garlic. Add the fennel, immediately turn up the heat and sauté for 5–6 minutes, stirring constantly. Add the eggplant, the Tabasco, and half the basil, and continue to sauté for 12–14 minutes, or until the eggplant is cooked. Add a little water during cooking to loosen the vegetables and the juices that will stick to the base. Then add the quartered tomatoes, season, and sauté for a further minute so the tomato softens only slightly. Invert onto a dish garnished with the remaining basil and shaved Parmesan.

VEGETABLE SAUTE

WITH POLENTA GNOCCHI

This is a simple meal with the soft and moist polenta poured on top of the vegetables and set briefly under a hot broiler. Finely shredded Parmesan and a drizzling of olive oil are all that's needed to make it delicious.

SERVES
6

INGREDIENTS

- 5 fl oz olive oil
- 2 cups red onions, cut into 4 or 6 pieces depending on size
- 2 garlic cloves, finely sliced
- dash of Tabasco
- ¾ lb fennel bulbs, cut into 2 in chunks
- 5 fl oz water
- ¾ lb eggplant, cut into 2 in chunks
- ¾ lb zucchini, cut into 1 in slices
- 1 red bell pepper, broiled, skinned, and cut into ½ in wide strips (see page 173)
- 6 tomatoes, blanched, skinned, cut into quarters and deseeded

- several leaves of basil
- large handful of washed baby spinach
- salt and freshly ground black pepper

FOR THE TOPPING

- 2½ cups polenta
- 1 quart salted boiling water
- ¾ cup dolcelatte cheese (optional)
- 1 tbsp olive oil
- ¾ cup Parmesan cheese, freshly shredded

METHOD

Heat the oil in a pan and add the chunks of red onion together with the garlic, a little salt and pepper, and a dash of Tabasco. Remove from the heat before they discolor. Then, in the same pan, sauté the fennel, adding a little of the water and seasoning until gently brown but still firm. Remove, then add the chunks of eggplant, and sauté so that they turn gold but retain their shape. Do the same with the zucchini.

Return all vegetables to the pan and add the red bell pepper and tomato and basil leaves. Toss over high heat for 4–5 minutes. Remove from heat and add the spinach and toss until just wilted. Place the vegetables in an ovenproof dish or 6 individual dishes.

Prepare the polenta according to the method on page 88. Stir in the dolcelatte if using, and pour the polenta over the vegetables. Lightly mark the top with a fork. Drizzle with olive oil and place under a hot broiler for 2–3 minutes until just beginning to crisp. Sprinkle generously with freshly shredded Parmesan and serve at once.

LAYERED BROILED VEGETABLE RING

This elegant dish looks good on buffet tables. It can be made a day or so in advance, covered and refrigerated, but be sure to serve warm or at room temperature.

SERVES
6 - 8

INGREDIENTS

- 1 lb mozzarella cheeses, cut into 8 slices
- 5 fl oz olive oil
- dash of Tabasco
- 3 garlic cloves, crushed
- 1 large eggplant, cut into ¼ in slices
- 2 fennel bulbs, cut into ¼ in slices
- 3 medium zucchini, cut lengthwise into thick slices
- 2 bunches scallions, trimmed
- 2 red and 2 yellow bell peppers, broiled, skinned, and each cut into 6 (see page 173)

- 1 tbsp balsamic vinegar
- salt and freshly ground black pepper
- basil leaves, for garnish

FOR THE SAUCE
- ½ cup olive oil
- ½ cup very red sundried tomato paste
- 5 tbsp warm water
- dash of Tabasco
- dash of balsamic vinegar
- a few small basil leaves

METHOD

Marinate the mozzarella slices in a third of the olive oil with salt, pepper, Tabasco, and some of the crushed garlic. Set aside.

Make the sauce by stirring the olive oil into the sundried tomato paste, then adding the warm water, Tabasco, vinegar, and seasoning. Set aside.

Preheat the broiler. Baste all the vegetables except the peppers with olive oil and sprinkle with salt, pepper, and the remaining crushed garlic. Lay the eggplant slices on a baking sheet and broil on both sides until well browned. Repeat with the fennel, then the zucchini and the scallions. Take care with the latter as they brown quickly.

Place all the vegetables in a bowl, add the balsamic vinegar, and let cool.

Layer the vegetables inside a 10 in ring mold. Begin with the eggplant slices, followed by the sliced mozzarella and the rest of the vegetables, completing with the zucchini and peppers laid in stripes on the final layer.

Place an upturned plate on top of the mold and turn so the plate is right-side up. Carefully remove the ring to reveal the many colors. Serve with the sauce and chunks of olive bread, green and black olives, and garnish with loosely scattered basil leaves.

SUNDAY ROAST

WITH ROASTED VEGETABLES,
AND MUSHROOM AND ONION SAUCE

A most traditional-looking roasted dinner, and one that we have served as the Cranks Christmas Special. If this doesn't seem like enough of a feast, you can also serve Baby Brussels sprouts (see page 154).

(see page 154)

SERVES
6

INGREDIENTS

- ¼ cup olive oil
- 1 lb onions, diced
- 3 garlic cloves, crushed
- 2 cups ground almonds
- 2 cups matzo meal
- ½ lb carrots, shredded
- 1 tsp bouillon powder
- 1 heaping tbsp parsley, finely chopped
- 1 heaping tbsp fresh cilantro leaves
- pinch of nutmeg
- 2 eggs, medium sized, beaten

FOR THE FILLING
- ¼ cup olive oil
- 1 cup onion, diced
- 1 cup prunes, pitted and soaked in water
- 1 garlic clove, finely chopped
- 1 tsp bouillon powder
- salt and freshly ground black pepper

METHOD

Heat the oil and sauté the onion and garlic until pale gold in color. Remove from heat and add all the other ingredients. Mix thoroughly with a wooden spoon and set aside.

Meanwhile, make the filling. Heat the olive oil and sauté the onion until brown. Add the soaked prunes and some of the water they have been soaking in. Simmer gently for about 10 minutes, adding the garlic and bouillon powder.

Preheat the oven to 400°F. Oil a sheet of foil 12 x 12 in and place the ground almond mixture at one end, shaping it into a long sausage about 4 inches in diameter and 12 in long. With your fingers, make a deep indentation that extends from one end to the other, and place the prune filling into it. Then bring the almond mixture round to enclose the filling, and press with your fingers to seal, smoothing with the palm of your hand as you go. Wrap tightly in the foil so that it does not dry out, and place in an ovenproof dish half filled with boiling water. Bake in the oven for 35 minutes until set to the touch.

Serve 2 slices of the almond and prune roll per person, with a square of the potatoes, the roasted carrots and parsnips, the Brussels sprouts, and the sauce.

INGREDIENTS

ROASTED PARSNIPS AND CARROTS

- 6 whole large carrots
- 6 whole large parsnips
- ¼ cup olive oil
- 2 garlic cloves, crushed
- salt and freshly ground black pepper

METHOD

Peel the carrots and parsnips and cut into 4 even-sized batons. Mix with all other ingredients and place in an ovenproof dish in the oven and roast with the almond and prune roll for 35 minutes until browned and tender.

INGREDIENTS

POTATOES

- 3 lb potatoes, finely sliced no more than ⅛ in thick
- 1 medium onion, very finely sliced
- 3 garlic cloves, crushed
- salt and freshly ground black pepper

METHOD

Mix the potatoes with the onion, garlic, salt, and pepper, and place in an ovenproof dish. Cover tightly with foil and bake in the preheated oven for 50 minutes until the potatoes are tender and golden brown on the bottom when inverted. Cut into neat squares for serving.

INGREDIENTS

FOR THE SAUCE

- 1 cup onions, diced
- ¼ cup olive oil
- 1 cup field, chestnut, or other dark mushrooms, roughly chopped
- 2 garlic cloves, finely crushed
- ¼ cup red wine
- 1 heaping tsp cornstarch
- salt and freshly ground black pepper

METHOD

Fry the onion in the olive oil until brown and add the roughly chopped mushrooms. Continue to sauté for a couple of minutes and add the garlic and red wine. Dissolve the cornstarch in a little cold water and stir into the sauce. Bring back to a boil so that it just thickens. Season to taste.

NOTE

Set the oven at 400°F for all the vegetables.

FILLED FIELD MUSHROOMS

WITH PUY LENTILS

It is often a challenge to use ingredients whose colors and texture are reminiscent of the earth without ending up with dull and unappetizing dishes. Yet here is a dish which, while satisfying the appetite, is colorful and contemporary.

SERVES

6

INGREDIENTS

- 1 lb Puy lentils
- 3 cups water
- 1 sprig fresh basil
- juice of ½ lime, plus ½ lime to add to lentils
- 4 garlic cloves
- 6 large open cap mushrooms
- 4 tbsp olive oil
- 3–4 tbsp tamari
- dash of Tabasco

- 1 fennel bulb, chopped
- 1 tbsp brandy
- 1 red and 1 yellow bell pepper, broiled, peeled, and cut into strips (see page 173)
- 1 tbsp balsamic vinegar
- 1 cup baby spinach
- 1 handful fresh cilantro, roughly chopped
- ¾ cup yogurt
- salt and freshly ground black pepper

METHOD

Place the lentils in a pan of cold water and bring to a boil. Do not add salt at this stage as this inhibits the cooking process, but add a sprig of fresh basil, half a lime cut into quarters, and two peeled garlic cloves. Simmer gently for 35–40 minutes until the lentils are tender but still firm.

Meanwhile, remove the stalks from the mushrooms, chop, and set aside. Sauté the whole mushroom caps for 5 minutes in 3 tbsp of olive oil, 1 tsp of tamari, a dash of Tabasco, and a clove of crushed garlic. Remove from heat and reserve any juices that may be left in the pan.

Sauté the fennel in 1 tbsp of olive oil and half a crushed garlic clove, and when tender, add the chopped mushroom stalks. Add the cooked lentils, reserved mushroom liquor, brandy, and remaining tamari.

Sauté the pepper strips briefly in an almost dry sautéing pan with the balsamic vinegar, then add the spinach. Fold into the lentil mixture and fill each of the mushrooms generously.

Finally, add the scant juice of half a lime, the remaining crushed garlic, the cilantro leaves, and a little salt and pepper to the yogurt and serve a spoonful of it with each filled mushroom.

BUTTERBEAN CASSEROLE WITH CIDER

The golden rules when cooking dried beans are: Do not undercook and do not overcook. A butterbean, a chickpea, a haricot bean, or a flageolet must be soft and with no trace of a white, hard center, and yet should be whole and not reduced to soup. Dried beans should not be salted during the cooking process–the salt prevents them from going soft–but once cooked, do not be stingy with it. Make sure that when you cook dried beans, they simmer slowly, with enough oil and sufficient spicing to render them rich, delicious, and succulent. You can then indulge in some of the oldest known dishes, enjoying the chanas of India, the hariras of Morocco, the minestrones of Italy, and the baked beans of America.

INGREDIENTS

- 4 cups dried butterbeans, soaked overnight
- 2½ cups onions, diced
- 3 garlic cloves, crushed
- ½ cup olive oil
- 1½ cups carrots, cut into 1 in chunks
- dash of tamari
- ½ cup hard cider
- ½ lb zucchini, cut into 1 in chunks
- 1¼ cups button mushrooms
- 1 cup corn kernels, frozen or taken off the cob
- handful of fresh basil
- handful of fresh cilantro
- salt and freshly ground black pepper

METHOD

Boil the butterbeans in plenty of water until they are tender but still intact.

Meanwhile, sauté the onion and garlic in the heated olive oil until pale gold in color. Add the chunks of carrots and continue to sauté for a minute or two, adding a little tamari and some of the hard cider. Then add the zucchini and sauté for a further minute so that they don't lose their color. Add the mushrooms, sauté for a few minutes, adding a little more tamari and a little more hard cider, as well as salt and pepper to taste. Finally, add the corn and continue to stir. Add the cooked butterbeans with a little of the liquid they have cooked in, and simmer gently for a further 10 minutes, adding the remaining hard cider so that all the flavors come together. Mix with plenty of freshly chopped basil and cilantro, and serve.

PAN-FRIED NOODLES
WITH SEARED BEAN CURD, VEGETABLES,
AND CASHEW NUTS

An Asian-inspired meal in a wok: The sizzling and searing and
the multitude of smells will make you want to eat a very
large bowl of this. Some touches, such as the broiled and
skinned peppers, are Mediterranean of course, as is the
addition of balsamic vinegar.

I have a cheap but lethal vegetable slicing machine, with a
julienne attachment to cut all manner of vegetables into
perfect matchsticks. Without this, or a similar attachment in
a food processor, you will have to cut the zucchini and carrots
into matchsticks by hand.

SERVES

6

INGREDIENTS

- ½ cup olive oil
- 2 tsp sesame oil
- ¾ cup carrots, cut into thin julienne strips
- ¾ cup zucchini, cut into thin julienne strips
- 1 red and 1 yellow bell pepper, charbroiled and skinned (see page 173), then cut into neat ¼ in strips with all the white pith removed
- ½ cup snowpeas
- 1 cup baby corn
- 1 cup leeks, sliced finely on the slant
- ½ cup eggplant, cut into thin julienne strips
- 1 tsp Tabasco
- 3 tbsp tamari
- 1 tbsp Ume-Su (see page 152)
- 1 tbsp balsamic vinegar

- 1 tsp freshly shredded ginger or galangal
- 2 garlic cloves, crushed
- ½ fiery red chili pepper, very finely sliced
- large handful of cilantro leaves, picked off the stalks, half reserved for garnish
- 4 oz smoked bean curd, cut into thin strips
- ¼ cup cashew nuts
- 1½ lb thick egg noodles, cooked
- 1 egg, beaten
- 5 tbsp sesame seeds

TO GARNISH

- 2 scallions, sliced finely on the slant
- 1 heaping tbsp chives, neatly and finely chopped,

METHOD

Heat a little of the olive and sesame oils in a wok and sauté the carrots for less than a minute so that they remain *al dente*. Remove from the heat and sauté each of the vegetables in turn, seasoning with the Tabasco, tamari, Ume-Su, balsamic vinegar, ginger, garlic, chili pepper, and half of the cilantro as you go. Regularly moisten the pan with water to loosen the juices which adhere to it but only add a drop of oil when absolutely necessary and only between vegetables. Sauté the bean curd strips until gold and crisp and reserve some for garnish.

In an almost completely dry pan, toast the cashew nuts until they are golden brown and charred in places. Set aside.

Now return all the stir-fried ingredients and the noodles to the pan and continue to sauté for a couple of minutes.

Remove from the heat and stir in the beaten egg. Use a fork to twist a separate serving onto each plate, and garnish liberally with toasted cashews, sesame seeds, scallion, chives, the reserved bean curd strips, and cilantro.

NOODLES

WITH PUMPKIN, COCONUT MILK, CILANTRO, AND FRESH CHILI PEPPER

I cannot imagine that there was once a time when cilantro was frowned upon, even sneered at, when coconut milk was as dimly known as the exotic and far-off land from which it hails, and eating chili peppers a daredevil act for drunken men. Three cheers for culinary expansion: This dish is a triumph of flavors and easier to make than pie.

SERVES
6

INGREDIENTS

- 1 lb pumpkin, cut into 1 in chunks
- 1 cup carrots, cut into 1 in slices
- ½ cup corn oil
- 3 garlic cloves, crushed
- dash of Tabasco
- 1½ cups zucchini, cut into 1 in slices
- 1 cup onions, diced
- 1½ lb Udon or egg noodles
- 1¼ cups coconut milk
- handful of fresh cilantro
- ½ fresh chili pepper, sliced very finely
- salt and freshly ground black pepper

METHOD

Preheat the oven to 425°F.

Place the pumpkin chunks, carrots, and 3 tbsp of the oil in an ovenproof dish. Add a little crushed garlic, salt and pepper, and a dash of Tabasco. Repeat with the zucchini in a separate dish as they will take slightly less time to cook. Place the pumpkin in the preheated oven and roast for 20–25 minutes until browned and tender. If there's room in your oven, roast the zucchini at the same time, but check them after about 10 minutes and remove when browned. Alternatively, roast the zucchini after the pumpkin.

Meanwhile, sauté the onion in the remaining oil until golden and set aside. Cook the noodles in plenty of salted boiling water, drain, and set aside.

When the vegetables are cooked, add to the fried onion and pour in the coconut milk. Simmer gently for 2 minutes, and add the fresh cilantro and chili pepper, reserving some of each for garnishing. Add the noodles, stir, and serve at once with a garnish of fresh cilantro and chili pepper.

RATATOUILLE

This is my version of ratatouille made without tomatoes.
In this recipe, the bright red comes from the vibrant color of
the best quality sweet paprika, slowly cooked in fragrant olive
oil. The zucchini and peppers can stay quite firm.

SERVES

6

INGREDIENTS

- ½ cup olive oil
- 1 lb (generous) eggplant, cut into 1–1¼ in chunks
- about 1¼ cups water
- 1 tbsp paprika
- 4 garlic cloves, crushed
- dash of Tabasco
- 2 cups zucchini, cut into 1 in slices
- 1 red bell pepper, ½ yellow bell pepper and ½ green bell pepper, each cut into 2 in neat squares
- salt and freshly ground black pepper

METHOD

Heat the olive oil in a large pan. Add the eggplant and sauté for 8–10 minutes, adding a little of the water if it begins to stick to the pan. Add the paprika, crushed garlic, and Tabasco. Then add the zucchini and sauté until they begin to go soft and the eggplant dissolves in parts to form the basis of a sauce. Continue to simmer gently for 8–10 minutes, covering with a lid but stirring at regular intervals. Finally, add the chunks of pepper and a little more water if necessary, continuing to sauté the vegetables for about 5–6 minutes over high heat until the peppers have just begun to soften but retain their color. The sauce should be thick and red from the paprika, so add water only to loosen the juices from the bottom of the pan and to make a paste with the slowly dissolving eggplant. Some of the eggplant must, however, remain intact.

Ratatouille is better when the flavors have been allowed to develop, so you may wish to remove it from the heat, let it cool, and heat it through again just before serving with large chunks of warm bread, a simple baked potato, or small new potatoes tossed in olive oil.

FILLED PEPPERS

WITH YOGURT AND CILANTRO SALSA

Filled peppers are delicious, especially if the peppers are roasted first and the filling is kept as fresh and crisp as possible. Canned cannellini beans work well in this filling.

SERVES
6

INGREDIENTS

- 6 whole red bell peppers
- 3 garlic cloves, crushed
- 1 cup red onions, diced
- 1 tbsp olive oil
- 1 lb zucchini, diced into ½ in pieces
- 1 tsp grain mustard
- dash of Tabasco
- 1½ cups cooked cannellini beans
- few leaves of fresh basil, chopped
- sprig of fresh cilantro, chopped
- sprig of fresh parsley, chopped

- ¼ cup scallion, chopped
- salt and freshly ground black pepper

FOR THE SALSA

- 1¼ cups plain or Greek yogurt
- 6 tbsp water
- 2 scallions, neatly and finely chopped
- handful of fresh cilantro, chopped
- 1 garlic clove, crushed
- 1 tsp cumin (optional)

METHOD

Preheat the broiler. Place the whole peppers on a baking sheet with a very light sprinkling of salt and pepper and a crushed clove of garlic. Place under the hot broiler, turning frequently so that the skins just begin to char all the way round. Let cool, then remove the tops, seeds, and pith. Set aside.

To make the salsa, mix all the ingredients together and set aside.

Sauté the red onion for 1–2 minutes in the heated olive oil so that it retains its color. Add the diced zucchini, remaining crushed garlic, grain mustard, and Tabasco and sauté for a further 5 minutes. Add the cannellini beans, and stir carefully. Add the chopped herbs and the chopped scallion. Fill each pepper generously, and serve with the salsa.

KUMARA PIE

Kumara is the Maori name for sweet potatoes and this is a dish that has found its way onto New Zealand menus. The layering effect is the same as for Gratin Dauphinois, but there is no cheese and the potatoes crisp up and caramelize in their own sugars. I find the combination of sour cream and heavy cream works to rich perfection, but it is equally possible with only one or the other. The garam masala and nutmeg are subtle additions which do not mask the sweetness of the potatoes.

INGREDIENTS

- 2 lb sweet potatoes
- 2 tbsp butter
- 1 cup onions, very finely sliced into rings
- 2 cups sour cream
- 5 fl oz heavy cream

- 1 level tsp garam masala
- large pinch of nutmeg
- 1 garlic clove, crushed
- salt and freshly ground black pepper

METHOD

Preheat the oven to 350°F.

Peel the potatoes, removing any black eyes. Cut into ¼ in thick slices. Rub the sides of an ovenproof dish with a little of the butter and cut the rest into small cubes. Mix all ingredients together and spread evenly into the dish. Place in the preheated oven and cook for at least 1 hour until the potatoes are soft and some are beginning to go crisp and brown on top.

Serve with a simple watercress salad, lightly dressed with a touch of lemon and a light olive oil.

BOSTON BAKED BEANS

Like my ratatouille on page 126, this is another example of
a dish whose red hue owes everything to paprika and nothing
at all to tomatoes.

Like my ratatouille on page 126

SERVES
8

INGREDIENTS

- 3 cups dried fava beans, soaked overnight
- 1½ lb onions, diced
- 6 tbsp olive oil
- 1 heaping tbsp paprika
- 3 garlic cloves, crushed
- 3 cups water

- ¼ cup molasses
- dash of Tabasco
- 10 vegetarian sausages, sliced
- 1 tbsp finely chopped parsley
- salt and freshly ground black pepper

METHOD

Place the fava beans in a pan, cover with water, and bring to a boil. Cook for about 1
hour until nearly tender, then drain.

Sauté the onion in two-thirds of the oil until golden brown, then add two-thirds of
the paprika and the crushed garlic. Sauté for 4–5 minutes, then add the beans and the
water. Bring back to a simmer. Cover with a lid and stir occasionally, cooking until the
beans are soft, which may take up to 1¹/₂ hours. You may complete this stage of the
cooking in a pressure cooker which will take considerably less time (about 15–20
minutes). Add the molasses, Tabasco, and salt and pepper to taste.

Meanwhile, heat the rest of the oil, add the remaining paprika, and sauté the sausages
until they are crisp and brown on both sides. Add to the beans and simmer for a further
7–8 minutes. Garnish with a little finely chopped parsley and serve.

savory tarts

Crisp, golden pastry packed with innovative and mouth-wateringly good fillings: The savory tarts in this chapter are light years away from the sad and sorry quiches found in the supermarket's frozen food section.

Few dishes have suffered the inequities of the quiche. I found it hard to use the word when writing this chapter as it so often refers to the sad imitations that still fill deli shelves and the supermarket's frozen food section. Instead, imagine light, crisp, melting pastry, made with butter and Parmesan and fresh herbs. Imagine a soft, rich, creamy filling using many different vegetables.

A successful tart needs to be made in a shallow, loose-bottomed pan that has been well floured and buttered. The pie dough should be rolled out thinly, laid inside the pan, pressed against the sides, and then pricked all over with a fork. Chill the pie shell for at least 30 minutes. Bake the shell first until it is pale gold and crispy, and let cool slightly before adding the filling and baking again. If you use an egg-based filling, make sure that you bake it only until it is just set and light golden in color.

CHERRY TOMATO TART
WITH FETA CHEESE AND BLACK OLIVES

A pretty summer tart, which is just as good hot or cold. It is best made in a fluted rectangular pan. The feta cheese and black olives are both so salty that you will need no additional salt.

SERVES

6

INGREDIENTS

FOR THE PIE DOUGH
- 1½ cups all purpose flour, sifted
- pinch of salt
- 6 tbsp butter, diced
- ½ cup Gruyère or Parmesan cheese, shredded
- 1 egg yolk, medium sized

FOR THE FILLING
- 2 cups feta cheese, crumbled
- 1⅓ cups black olives. pitted and chopped
- 2 heaping tbsp basil, roughly chopped, plus whole leaves for garnish
- 1 lb cherry tomatoes

METHOD

To make the pie dough, place the flour, salt, and butter on a board or in a large bowl and rub lightly with your fingers until the mixture resemble fine bread crumbs. Stir in the cheese. Mix the egg yolk with about 2 tbsp of very cold water and add to the flour. Bring together with a circular motion of your opened-out fingers and invert onto a lightly floured board. Knead for 5–6 minutes until smooth, then wrap in plastic wrap and refrigerate for about 20 minutes.

Meanwhile, mash the crumbled feta cheese together with the chopped olives and add the chopped basil. Set aside.

Butter and flour a rectangular pan, 14 x 4½ in. Roll out the pie dough onto a lightly floured surface. Line the pan with the dough and prick all over with a fork. Set aside for 30 minutes, preferably in the fridge.

Preheat the oven to 400°F. Bake the pie shell in the preheated oven for 10 minutes or until golden brown. Let cool slightly, then spread the feta and olive mixture evenly all over the bottom of the pie shell. Arrange the tomatoes on top and return to the oven for 15 minutes until the skins have burst and the tomatoes look slightly shrivelled in places. Garnish with the whole basil leaves before serving.

BROCCOLI AND DOLCELATTE TART

WITH MASCARPONE

The tart is loosely covered with waxed paper before baking, which prevents the broccoli from going black. The mascarpone combined with the dolcelatte results in a more delicate tart than you might expect.

SERVES
8

INGREDIENTS

- 1 lb broccoli
- prebaked pie shell (see page 135)
- 6 eggs, medium sized
- 2 cups mascarpone cheese
- 1½ cups dolcelatte cheese
- salt and freshly ground black pepper

METHOD

Preheat the oven to 425°F. Separate the broccoli into flowerets and blanch in a pan of salted boiling water for 2 minutes. Drain well, then arrange in the pie shell. Beat the eggs, mascarpone, and dolcelatte together in a bowl with a hand-held mixer. Add salt and freshly ground black pepper, and pour all over the broccoli and into the gaps. Cover loosely with waxed paper as mentioned above, and bake for 20–25 minutes or until just set, and serve.

NADINE'S PISSALADIERE

A traditional pissaladière from the south of France is usually made with a yeast dough and has anchovies on it. Because it is said to be a cross between a quiche and a pizza, I played around with it and came up with this version which could more properly be called a quichaladière. It is essential that the tomato sauce is very well reduced.

SERVES
8

INGREDIENTS

FOR THE PIE DOUGH
- I cup butter, diced
- I cup all purpose white flour, sifted
- I cup all purpose wholewheat flour, sifted
- pinch of salt
- ice-cold water

FOR THE FILLING
- I large onion, sliced
- ¼ cup olive oil

- 4 cups canned, whole, peeled tomatoes
- 3 garlic cloves, left whole
- pinch of brown sugar
- ½ cup sundried tomatoes in oil, chopped
- handful of basil, left whole
- 2 cups black olives, pitted and chopped
- 3 eggs, medium sized
- 6 tbsp heavy cream
- ½ cup Gruyère or smoked Cheddar, shredded
- salt and freshly ground black pepper

METHOD

Make the dough by rubbing the butter into the flours and salt until it resembles fine crumbs. Add a little water and bring together to form a smooth dough. Wrap and refrigerate for 20 minutes.

Meanwhile, make the tomato sauce by sautéing the onion in the hot olive oil until soft, then adding the canned tomatoes, peeled garlic cloves, sugar, sundried tomatoes, and whole basil leaves. Cook for 40 minutes, stirring regularly, until reduced to a thick consistency with no runny liquid. Retrieve the garlic and whole basil leaves and discard.

Preheat the oven to 425°F. Butter and flour a 10 in loose-bottomed tart pan. Roll out the dough, and line the pan. Prick all over with a fork and bake in the preheated oven for 15 minutes until pale gold in color.

Spread the chopped olives evenly over the pie shell and follow with a layer of tomato sauce. Beat the eggs, cream, and cheese together and add a little salt and coarsely ground black pepper. Use a fork to make holes all over the olive and tomato layers (so that the custard can sink in) and pour over the egg mixture.

Return to the oven and bake for 15–20 minutes or until the top is gently set. A little runniness at this stage is acceptable as the custard will continue to set in its own heat once you have taken the tart out of the oven. Serve hot or warm.

MUSHROOM LATTICE TART

You could also make this as individual tartlets. A few wild mushrooms are all that's needed to create a deep and earthy flavor. Tamari, as usual, brings out the mushroom flavor perfectly and tarragon has long been associated with mushrooms, though if you find it too sweet, you could replace it with fresh thyme.

SERVES

8

INGREDIENTS

- 2 tbsp butter
- 8 cups button or chestnut mushrooms, sliced
- 1 cup dried wild mushrooms, soaked in a little hot water to reconstitute, and drained
- 3 garlic cloves, crushed
- large sprig fresh tarragon
- 1 tbsp tamari
- 1 tbsp brandy
- salt and freshly ground black pepper

- double quantity pie dough (see page 135), half used to make the prebaked pie shell and half reserved for lattice top
- beaten egg, to glaze

FOR THE SAUCE

- ¾ cup milk
- 2 tbsp butter
- ¼ cup all purpose flour

METHOD

Preheat the oven to 425°F. Melt the butter in a saucepan over low heat and add the mushrooms, the crushed garlic, tarragon, salt, and pepper. Sauté for about 5 minutes. Add the tamari and the brandy and continue to sauté for a couple of minutes. Strain and reserve the liquor.

For the sauce, warm the milk until just before boiling point. Melt the butter in another pan over medium heat. Add the flour and stir thoroughly until completely amalgamated and the mixture comes away from the sides of the pan. Slowly pour in the warm milk, stirring the whole time. Complete by adding the reserved mushroom liquor. Stir well and mix with the mushrooms.

Spread the mushroom mixture evenly over the prebaked pie shell and make the lattice by rolling out the remaining dough and cutting out 14 strips, each ½ in wide. Interweave them over the filling exactly as in the Dutch Apple Pie (see page 248). Lightly glaze the dough with beaten egg and bake for 30 minutes until golden brown. Serve hot or warm.

GARLIC, OLIVE, AND BROILED ZUCCHINI TART

The boiled garlic gives this a pronounced, sweet garlic taste which is quite refined. Use a good full-looking head of garlic. A version of this tart was first made by Suzanne Cullen, who now runs Culinary Arts for Cranks.

SERVES
8

INGREDIENTS

- prebaked pie shell (see page 135)
- 1½ lb zucchini, sliced into ¼ in slices
- 1 fl oz olive oil
- dash of Tabasco
- 1 garlic clove, crushed
- 1–2 garlic heads, left whole
- 6 eggs, medium sized
- 1 cup heavy cream
- ½ cup green and black olives, pitted and roughly chopped
- salt and freshly ground black pepper

METHOD

Baste the zucchini slices with olive oil, a little salt, Tabasco, and the crushed garlic. Place under a hot broiler and broil for 7 minutes on each side or until browned.

Preheat the oven to 425°F. Meanwhile, bring a small pan of salted water to a boil and blanch the whole garlic for 7 minutes or until soft. Remove from the pan. Peel and scoop out the flesh.

Place the eggs, cream, garlic flesh, salt, and pepper in a bowl and whisk briefly with a hand-held electric mixer. Stir in half of the roughly chopped olives. Pour into the pre-baked pie shell and then arrange the zucchini and the remaining olives all over. Baked for 15–20 minutes or until set but still moist. Serve hot or warm.

FRENCH ONION TART

A classic and simple tart that remains one of the very best.
The onions need to be very well browned, but must not go
black. Adding a tablespoon of port or marsala wine in
addition to the tamari makes the flavor richer and sweeter.
You might like to experiment using red onions.

INGREDIENTS

- prebaked pie shell (see page 135)
- ¼ cup olive oil
- 2 lb onions, finely sliced
- 3 garlic cloves, crushed
- pinch of freshly ground nutmeg
- 1 tbsp marsala wine

- 1 tbsp tamari
- 5 eggs, medium sized
- 5 fl oz heavy cream
- ½ cup Gruyère cheese, shredded
- salt and freshly ground black pepper

METHOD

Heat the oil and gently sauté the onion and garlic, seasoned with salt, freshly ground
black pepper, and some freshly grated nutmeg, for about 40 minutes or until a dark
golden brown. Raise the heat and add the marsala wine and the tamari and sauté for a
further 5 minutes, stirring all the time.

Preheat the oven to 425°F. Spread the onion mixture evenly over the pie shell. Beat
the eggs with the heavy cream and add in the cheese and a little more nutmeg and salt.
Pour over the onion filling, making holes in the onion layer to allow the egg mixture to
seep through. Bake in the preheated oven for 20–25 minutes or until set but still moist.

ROASTED BABY EGGPLANT TART

This must classify as one of the prettiest tarts of all, and it is even prettier baked in a heart-shaped pan. Make it for a romantic meal and serve it with champagne, by candlelight.

SERVES
8 – 10

INGREDIENTS

- prebaked pie shell (see page 135)
- 1 lb baby eggplant, cut in half
- ¼ cup olive oil
- 3 garlic cloves, crushed
- dash of Tabasco
- ½ cup cherry tomatoes
- ½ cup black olives, pitted

- handful fresh basil, the smallest leaves reserved for garnish
- 4 eggs, small
- 1 cup heavy cream
- ½ cup Parmesan cheese, freshly shredded
- salt and freshly ground black pepper

METHOD

Baste the eggplant halves generously in the olive oil, crushed garlic, and Tabasco, and season with salt and pepper. Place under a very hot broiler for 10 minutes, turning over at least once, until the cut side is a dark golden color and the skins are slightly charred.

Preheat the oven to 400°F.

Arrange the eggplant halves in the prebaked pie shell, cut side up. Fill the gaps with the cherry tomatoes, olives, and basil. Mix the eggs, cream, and Parmesan together and season. Pour all over, taking care to leave as much of the vegetables exposed as possible. Bake for 20–25 minutes or until set but still moist. Serve hot or warm.

GRILLED MEDITERRANEAN TART

The chunkiness of the vegetables and their vibrant colors, added to the fact that they are pre-roasted, gives this tart particular appeal. The eggs and cream act largely as a binder for the vegetables, which should be abundantly in evidence.

INGREDIENTS

- ¾ cup red bell pepper, cut into 1 in squares
- ¾ cup fennel, cut into 1½ in chunks
- ¾ cup tomatoes, cut into quarters
- ¾ cup zucchini, cut into ½ in slices
- 6 tbsp olive oil
- 3–4 garlic cloves, crushed
- dash of Tabasco
- 3 eggs, small, beaten
- 1 cup heavy cream
- prebaked pie shell (see page 135)
- salt and freshly ground black pepper

METHOD

Preheat the oven to 475°F.

Place the cut vegetables, olive oil, two-thirds of the crushed garlic, salt, and pepper, and a generous dash of Tabasco, in an ovenproof dish. Mix thoroughly, then bake in the preheated oven for 20 minutes or until charred and a little shrivelled in places.

Meanwhile, beat the eggs, heavy cream, and the remaining garlic together, season, and set aside.

Reduce the oven temperature to 425°F. Place the vegetables in the prebaked pie shell. Pour over the egg mixture and return to the oven for a further 20 minutes or until set. Serve hot or warm.

PUMPKIN TART

WITH WALNUTS, SPINACH, AND PARMESAN

An unusual use of roasted pumpkin in a moist, delicate cream and egg base. The more you can stack up the pumpkin in the pie shell, the better.

SERVES

8

INGREDIENTS

- 3 lb pumpkin, peeled and cut into 2 in pieces
- 3 tbsp olive oil
- 3 garlic cloves, crushed
- ½ lb fresh spinach
- ½ cup walnut pieces

- 6 eggs, medium sized
- 1¼ cups heavy cream
- ½ cup fresh Parmesan cheese, shredded
- prebaked pie shell (see page 135)
- salt and freshly ground black pepper

METHOD

Preheat the oven to 450°F.

Place the chunks of pumpkin in an ovenproof dish and baste with the olive oil, salt, pepper, and a little of the crushed garlic. Roast in the preheated oven for about 20 minutes or until browned on all sides.

Remove the pumpkin from the oven and reduce the heat to 350°F. Add the spinach to the pumpkin and mix thoroughly until wilted in the heat. Then add the walnut pieces. Put the eggs in a bowl and beat well. Add the heavy cream, the remaining crushed garlic, and salt and pepper. Finally, stack the pumpkin chunks and spinach in the pie shell. Pour the egg and cream mixture on top and in between the chunks but allow as much of the pumpkin to show through as possible. Bake for 20–25 minutes or until just set. Remove from oven while still moist and sprinkle with the freshly shredded Parmesan. Let cool for a few minutes, then eat immediately.

SWISS CHARD
AND RADICCHIO TART

If, to your mind, radicchio has always been a salad leaf too bitter to use in anything but small quantities amid a variety of more mild-mannered leaves, but you are nonetheless tempted by its unusual claret and burgundy colors, then you will be pleased with this recipe. Very gentle braising softens the flavors and provides a crisp contrast to the custard and the strong green of the chard. Garlic cooked in this way is also gentler and less pungent than when used raw and adds a welcome sweetness to these components.

SERVES
8 – 10

INGREDIENTS

- 2 tbsp butter
- 1 large handful Swiss chard, chopped
- 1 large radicchio, roughly torn
- 4 eggs, small
- 1 cup heavy cream
- 1 cup cottage cheese
- 5–6 garlic cloves, blanched in boiling water until soft, then peeled and mashed
- prebaked pie shell (see page 135)
- salt and freshly ground black pepper

METHOD

Preheat the oven to 400°F.

Melt the butter and sauté the chard for a few minutes until wilted. Add the radicchio and salt and pepper and sauté for a further 1–2 minutes, so it is softened but still retains its color.

Mix the eggs, cream, and cottage cheese together and add the mashed garlic. Arrange the braised vegetables in the pie shell and pour the egg mixture carefully on top, leaving as much of the vegetables exposed as possible. Bake for 20–25 minutes, or until set but still moist. Serve hot or warm.

vegetables &

side dishes

Inspired by world cuisines, this chapter celebrates the vegetable, from the humble cabbage enlivened with wild mushrooms, to Jerusalem artichokes roasted with red wine and Gruyère cheese and root vegetables baked in parchment.

You will see by looking at the recipes that they can accompany some of the main course recipes to make an extra special meal. For everyday cooking, serve them with a simple rice or pasta dish to make a perfectly delicious meal in themselves. I hope that they will inspire you to create your own.

For more ideas, draw on the cooking of Asia, the Middle East, and the Mediterranean countries: Regions with a long, rich history of vegetarian cooking. Go to your nearest large supermarket, look carefully into Greek and Pakistani shops, and examine the stalls in your local grocery store. Ask about the exotic-looking, sculptural things you will see there. Learn their names and how to prepare and cook them. And most importantly of all, experiment.

ROASTED BABY SQUASH
SERVED WITH GREEK YOGURT

Really, half a squash roasted in its own protective skin, soft as purée, is a meal in itself. And the spoonful of Greek yogurt is a cold luxury in between hot, sweet, garlicky mouthfuls.

SERVES
6

INGREDIENTS

- 3 squash, each approximately 2 lb in weight
- ¾ cup olive oil
- 1 tbsp tamari
- 12 garlic cloves, left whole
- ½ cup Greek yogurt
- handful of fresh cilantro leaves
- salt and freshly ground black pepper

METHOD

Preheat the oven to 400°F.

Cut each squash in half and remove the seeds and fibres. Make diagonal cuts into the flesh but not all the way to the skin. Baste with the olive oil and tamari on both sides, and season. Fill each half with the unpeeled garlic cloves and turn upside down on an oiled ovenproof dish. Bake in the preheated oven for about 40 minutes or until the flesh feels tender when poked with a fork.

Remove from the oven. Scoop out the flesh, place it in a serving dish, and mash roughly. Break open the garlic cloves, add the flesh to the squash, and mash again. Serve topped with a thick dollop of Greek yogurt, spiked with several cilantro leaves. Lightly sautéed green beans (or snowpeas, broccoli, or asparagus) are all you will need on the side.

SNOWPEAS, BABY CORN, AND ASPARAGUS
WITH TOASTED SEEDS AND HIZIKI SEAWEED

This is a quick vegetable stir-fry that can be served hot, cold, or anything in between. Serve it with Camargue red rice mixed with wild rice and, if you like seaweed, add a tablespoon of nori flakes to the rice before serving. If not, finely chopped fresh chives and roughly chopped fresh cilantro will add color and interest. Ume-su is a Japanese vinegar made from pickled umeboshi plums. It has a distinctive taste and is stocked by Japanese and natural food stores.

SERVES

6

INGREDIENTS

- 3 heaping tbsp pumpkin seeds
- 1 heaping tbsp sesame seeds
- ¼ lb young asparagus, trimmed
- 1 tbsp olive oil
- ½ lb baby corn
- ¼ lb snowpeas, topped and tailed
- 3 tbsp water

- 1–2 tsp tamari
- 1–2 tsp ume-su
- 1 piece fresh chili pepper, 1 in long, finely chopped
- large handful of hiziki seaweed, soaked in hot water and 3 tbsp tamari until tender, then drained
- salt

METHOD

Toast the seeds in a dry pan with some salt until they begin to pop and turn golden brown. Set aside.

Bring a small pan of salted water to a boil (a milk pan is large enough). Immerse the asparagus and boil for precisely 1 minute. Drain and set aside.

Heat the olive oil in a large skillet or wok. Add the baby corn and sauté for 3–4 minutes, tossing and turning all the time until they begin to wilt very slightly and to turn golden in places. Add the asparagus and continue to sauté for 30 seconds, then add the snowpeas, and sauté for a further minute or so. Tossing the pan about, quickly add the water, which will sizzle in the heat, the tamari, and ume-su. Finally, add the finely chopped chili pepper and the drained, and by now tender, seaweed. Remove from heat and add the toasted seeds. Serve hot or cold.

BABY BRUSSELS
WITH PARMESAN AND NEW POTATOES

Brussels sprouts are as much a part of an English Christmas as tinsel and carols, and though you may belong to the breed that exclaims in despair, "I hate Brussels sprouts," at the very least try this method. Brussels sprouts are one of very few vegetables I will still subject to boiling but, as you can see from the recipe, only briefly. Don't waste precious time on the older variety, but search instead for small young sprouts. A generous pat of butter, some crushed garlic, lots of Parmesan: This is an easy and quick dish which may keep Brussels sprouts on your Christmas menu for years to come.

SERVES

6

INGREDIENTS

- 1 lb smallest new potatoes (olive potatoes)
- 1 lb baby Brussels sprouts
- 2 tbsp butter
- 1 garlic clove, crushed
- ½ cup finely chopped parsley
- ½ cup Parmesan cheese
- salt and freshly ground black pepper

METHOD

Place the potatoes in a pan of cold salted water and bring to a boil. Ten minutes into the cooking time, add the trimmed and cleaned Brussels sprouts, and continue to boil for another 3–4 minutes. Remove from the heat and refresh under cold water.

Melt the butter in a saucepan and return the vegetables to the heat for 3–4 minutes, together with the garlic, and salt and pepper. Remove from heat and add the chopped parsley. Invert into a dish and garnish generously with fine shavings of Parmesan and freshly ground black pepper.

SPLIT BROWNED POTATOES

There are times when it is best to leave classics and favorite dishes well alone, and you may consider browned potatoes to be one such instance. Slicing them in this fashion, however, quite apart from looking pretty, adds to their crispiness because it increases the surface area exposed to sizzling oil.

SERVES

6

INGREDIENTS

- 2 lb baking potatoes
- ½ cup olive oil
- I sprig fresh rosemary, leaves stripped
- salt and freshly ground black pepper

METHOD

Preheat the oven to its highest setting.

Peel the potatoes and keep in cold water while you work. Make parallel slits into the potatoes, taking care not to cut all the way through to the bottom. Sprinkle with salt and pepper and place in an ovenproof dish with the oil and the fresh rosemary, basting the potatoes generously. Then bake for 1 hour, turning occasionally, so that the potatoes become crisp and golden on all sides.

BAKED VEGETABLES IN PARCHMENT

This is an unusual way of serving root vegetables which brings out their sweetness very gently. Opening the bags to reveal the different vegetables is a real treat, and especially pretty because the beets weep some of their vermilion juices over the other vegetables.

INGREDIENTS

- ½ lb celeriac
- ½ lb carrots
- ½ lb beets
- ½ lb Jerusalem artichokes
- ½ lb sweet potatoes
- ½ lb parsnips
- ½ lb new potatoes
- ½ lb baby onions, peeled
- 12 garlic cloves, unpeeled
- ¼ cup olive oil

- 1 tbsp white wine
- 1 tbsp tamari
- salt and freshly ground black pepper
- 6–8 sheets of parchment 8 x 8 in wide

TO SERVE

- 1 cup quark
- 3 garlic cloves, crushed
- handful of basil or other herb, finely chopped

METHOD

Preheat the oven to 375°F.

Scrub all the vegetables clean and cut all but the potatoes and the baby onions into 1¼ in cubes. Mix the cut vegetables, potatoes, onions, and garlic with the olive oil, white wine, tamari, and salt and pepper.

Divide the vegetables equally between the sheets of parchment, wrap around, folding the edges tightly together to form a bag, and place closely together on a baking sheet. Place in the preheated oven for 35–40 minutes. Serve the vegetables in their packets, straight from the oven, with a bowl of quark, richly seasoned with crushed garlic, salt and pepper, and herbs, and let people spoon some over their vegetables as needed.

BRAISED CABBAGE
WITH WILD MUSHROOMS

Can it be true? Boring old cabbage in the same mouthful as wild mushrooms? Yes, if you braise the cabbage first, use heavy cream, and give it a kick with grain mustard. You will actually taste it for the delicious vegetable it really is. Don't worry about it being soft: Soggy is the only condition you have to avoid. The commonest of white cabbages will do, though Savoy is a brighter, finer thing, and requires a little less cooking time.

Serve this with creamed potatoes on a cold winter's day and go for a long walk afterward.

INGREDIENTS

- 3 lb white cabbage
- I tsp bouillon powder mixed into ½ cup hot water
- 2½ fl oz olive oil
- 3 garlic cloves, finely sliced
- ½ cup heavy cream
- I tsp grain mustard

- handful of chives, finely sliced
- 3 cups chanterelle mushrooms
- 2 tbsp butter
- a few leaves of fresh tarragon
- I tbsp tamari
- I tbsp red wine or brandy
- salt and freshly ground black pepper

METHOD

Trim the cabbage and remove the outer leaves. Chop it roughly and place in a heavy-bottomed saucepan with the bouillon mixture, oil, two finely sliced garlic cloves, salt, and pepper. Cover with a lid and bring to a boil. Immediately lower the heat and braise gently for 20 minutes or until the cabbage is soft and tender and the liquid reduced by two-thirds. Add two-thirds of the cream and the mustard. Continue to simmer for just a few minutes, then remove the pan from the heat and add almost all of the chives.

Meanwhile, carefully clean the mushrooms. Melt the butter in a pan and sauté them for just 2–3 minutes with the remaining garlic, a little salt and pepper, and the tarragon. Add the remaining cream, the tamari, and the wine or brandy. Bring to a gentle bubble and immediately remove from the heat. Place the hot cabbage in a warmed dish and pour the mushrooms and sauce over, garnishing with the remaining chives.

ROASTED JERUSALEM ARTICHOKES

WITH RED WINE

Despite their knobbly and earthy appearance, Jerusalem artichokes can have a sweet and delicate flavor, especially when cooked slowly as in this gratin. They are also delicious in soups with lemon and saffron. In this recipe, you don't even need to peel them: Simply remove the coarser, knobbly bits. When preparing them, place them first in a bowl of cold water that has been acidulated with lemon juice to avoid discoloration. In this recipe, they absorb the red wine, tamari, and olive oil juices and become even richer and more succulent.

SERVES

6

INGREDIENTS

- 1¼ lb Jerusalem artichokes, cut in half
- ¼ cup red wine
- 3 tbsp olive oil
- 1 tbsp tamari
- 2 garlic cloves, crushed
- dash of Tabasco
- 1 cup Gruyère cheese, shredded (optional)
- handful of chives, finely chopped
- salt and freshly ground black pepper

METHOD

Preheat the oven to 400°F.

Mix together all the ingredients except the cheese and chives and place in an ovenproof dish. Place in the preheated oven for 1 hour 10 minutes, until the artichoke skins are withered, the flesh tender and succulent, and the juices have formed a rich and sticky sauce. Add the Gruyère if using, so that it melts in the heat of the artichokes and leaves a thread when lifted. Garnish with chives and serve with a mix of brown and wild rice, sautéed green beans and asparagus, and green salad.

PUMPKIN AND SNOWPEAS

WITH SEAWEED

Three ingredients with such pronounced colors can only make this dish exciting to look at, and what appeals to the eyes will not fail to whet the appetite. This is another simple vegetable combination that is as healthy and nourishing as you could wish. Serve this with simply prepared lemon rice and one other broiled or roasted vegetable dish. Butternut or acorn squash also works well in this recipe.

SERVES

6

INGREDIENTS

- handful of hiziki seaweed
- about 5 tbsp tamari
- 3 garlic cloves, crushed
- dash of Tabasco
- ½ cup light olive oil
- 1¾ lb pumpkin, peeled and cut into 1¼ in chunks

- 1 piece ginger 1½ in, peeled and finely minced
- ⅓ lb snowpeas, cleaned
- small handful of fresh cilantro leaves
- 1 piece fresh coconut
- 1 piece chili pepper, very finely chopped

METHOD

Place the seaweed in a bowl with half the tamari, a little of the garlic, and a few drops of Tabasco. Cover with hot water and set aside until soft. Heat all but 1 tbsp of the oil gently, and add the pumpkin. Stir-fry for 3–4 minutes with most of the remaining garlic, most of the ginger, and a little Tabasco, turning over constantly with a wooden spoon, until the chunks begin to soften on the outside and to mingle with the seasonings. Then add all but 1 tsp of the remaining tamari, a little at a time, taking care that it does not stick and burn. Add a little water if necessary.

Heat the remaining oil in a separate pan and very quickly sauté the snowpeas with the reserved 1 tsp tamari, and the remaining garlic and ginger, letting them stay as green as possible. Add to the pumpkin. Drain the seaweed and add, along with most of the cilantro. Place on a large plate and, using a metal cheese slicer, very finely slice the coconut so that it falls over the vegetables like a mass of petals. Garnish with the remaining cilantro and the chili pepper, and serve immediately.

MIXED SQUASHES SAUTEED

WITH A FRESH HERB, GINGER, AND LIME GLAZE

This dish is probably best made when you have a large crowd to feed, so that you can make the most of the many kinds of squash now available in most supermarkets. Cutting the squashes into pieces makes them much easier to peel.

SERVES
6 – 8

INGREDIENTS

- 1 acorn squash
- 1 butternut squash
- 1 lb pumpkin
- 10 oz pattypan squash
- ¼ cup olive oil
- 4 tbsp butter

- 1 heaping tsp ground ginger
- zest and juice of 1 lime
- 1 tbsp brown sugar
- dash of Tabasco
- sprig of fresh sage, leaves chopped

METHOD

Cut the acorn squash, butternut squash, and pumpkin into manageable segments, removing the seeds, fibres and peel. Cut all the squashes into 1 in chunks. Bring a large pan of salted water to a boil. Add the squashes and simmer gently for 5–10 minutes, or until tender.

Meanwhile, place the olive oil and butter in a large pan, and heat gently until the butter melts. Add the ground ginger, lime juice, and sugar, and cook for 2 minutes until the sugar has completely dissolved. Add the Tabasco, sage, and lime zest, stir for 30 seconds, and then add the cooked squash. Heat through and serve at once with couscous and green salad.

TEMPURA GREEN BEANS

These are perfect either as a starter or served at a drinks party. The trick is to sauté them at the last moment to keep the batter light and crisp. Part of the water in the batter can be replaced by very cold beer, which will give a more interesting flavor.

INGREDIENTS

- I quart corn oil, for deep-frying
- I lb green beans, cleaned and blanched for I minute
- salt

FOR THE BATTER
- I large egg, separated
- 1½ cups very cold water
- I cup all purpose flour
- pinch of salt

FOR THE DIPPING SAUCE
- 6 tbsp tamari
- ¼ cup ume-su (see page 152)
- ¼ cup pickled daikon or pickled ginger, cut into fine strips
- dash of Tabasco

METHOD

Line a plate with several layers of paper towel. To make the dipping sauce, mix all the ingredients together and set aside.

To make the batter, mix the egg yolk with the cold water, sift the flour and salt into it, and mix lightly. Then lightly whisk the egg white and add just one half of it to the mixture. Discard the rest.

Heat the oil until it is very hot and then turn the heat down. Immerse a few green beans at a time into the batter and then drop them carefully into the hot oil. As soon as they crisp up and rise to the surface (less than a minute), remove them with two forks or a pair of tongs, place them on the paper towels, and sprinkle with salt while they are still very hot. Continue until all the green beans are fried.

Serve the green beans immediately, with the sauce in small bowls or ramekins, so people can dip the beans themselves.

THREE BEAN AND VEGETABLE PUREES

These vegetable purées are extremely versatile. They are excellent as spreads in sandwiches and on toast. They're also incredibly easy to make and several kinds on a buffet table look and taste great. The secret is in the olive oil, which should be extra virgin if possible, and in all the bits and pieces you add to them.

I used to shell the fava beans until I tested the recipe for this book and discovered that blending them longer removed this chore. The final result is still as bright and soft as spring leaves.

INGREDIENTS

FOR THE FAVA BEAN PUREE
- 1 lb fava beans, fresh or frozen
- ¼ cup extra virgin olive oil, plus 1 tbsp to garnish
- 2 garlic cloves, crushed
- ½ tsp cumin
- 1 scallion, very finely sliced
- salt and freshly ground black pepper

FOR THE CANNELLINI BEAN PUREE
- 2 cups canned cannellini beans
- 1 tbsp olive oil
- ½ cup sundried tomatoes in oil, thinly sliced
- ½ cup black olives, pitted and roughly chopped
- few basil leaves
- salt and freshly ground black pepper

FOR THE ROOT VEGETABLE PUREE
- 2 cups light vegetable stock
- 2 tbsp butter
- ¾ lb carrots, cut into ½ in chunks
- ¾ lb parsnips, cut into ½ in chunks
- ¾ lb celeriac or rutabaga, cut into ½ in chunks
- salt and freshly ground black pepper
- 4 tbsp chopped parsley or cilantro

METHOD

To make the fava bean purée, bring a pan of salted water to a boil, and boil the beans for 5–6 minutes or until tender. Place in a food processor on its highest speed and blend for 8–10 minutes until absolutely smooth, slowly adding the olive oil, crushed garlic, salt and pepper, and cumin as you do so. Transfer to a shallow bowl, pour the 1 tbsp olive oil on top, and garnish with the finely sliced scallion.

To make the cannellini bean purée, drain the beans and place in a food processor. Blend at high speed for a few seconds, adding the olive oil, and salt and pepper at the same time. Transfer to a shallow bowl, and fold in the slivers of sundried tomatoes and the olives. Garnish with the basil leaves.

To make the root vegetable purée, heat the stock until just boiling and set aside. Melt the butter in a heavy-bottomed saucepan and add the vegetables all in one go. Stir regularly for 5 minutes, then add the hot stock. Bring back to a boil and simmer gently for 25 minutes, covered with a lid. Check regularly that the vegetables are not sticking to the bottom of the pan and add a little more stock or water if necessary. Should there be any stock left by the time the vegetables are tender, strain it, and drink as it is or reserve for soup. Place the vegetables in a food processor and blend as smooth or as coarse as you like. Serve with a pat of butter and the chopped parsley or cilantro.

GRILLED SHIITAKE MUSHROOMS
WITH SCALLIONS

Funny how something you might describe as chewy and slippery can turn out to be so delicious. Shiitake mushrooms, Japanese par excellence, yet commercially available thanks to cultivating prowess, are delicious in all manner of Oriental dishes. They require just the briefest application of heat: A couple of minutes at most under a hot broiler is all that is needed here. With an equally brief broiling of scallions, this is a quick and sophisticated accompaniment. I like this served Oriental style, with several other vegetable dishes, each in its own bowl, each seasoned with individuality.

SERVES

6

INGREDIENTS

- 6 cups shiitake mushrooms
- 6 tbsp olive oil
- 1 tbsp teriyaki sauce
- small piece fresh chili pepper, very finely chopped
- 2 garlic cloves, finely chopped
- 12 scallions

- 6 tbsp water
- 4 tbsp peanut butter
- dash of Tabasco
- handful of fresh cilantro, some reserved for garnish

METHOD

Simply remove the toughest bits of the stalk from the mushrooms. Mix the olive oil, teriyaki sauce, most of the chili pepper and garlic together into a sauce, and brush the mushrooms with the sauce. Trim the scallions of their hairy tails and baste with the same sauce. Place under a hot broiler for a couple of minutes, turning over at least once, until charred and softened.

Add the water to the peanut butter and stir to dissolve, adding the remaining garlic and chili pepper, Tabasco, and cilantro. Warm gently and serve with the mushrooms and scallions, garnished with cilantro leaves.

ROASTED WINTER VEGETABLES

These roasted winter vegetables are substantial enough to form the main part of a meal and are so easy to prepare that I have sometimes placed them in the oven, gone shopping, and returned to a ready meal. Cubes of marinated plain or smoked bean curd can be separately roasted for 20 minutes and added to the vegetables. Some of the vegetables will cook faster than others. The mushrooms, for instance, will become quite shrivelled, but as long as they don't burn you will find this simply intensifies their flavor. Various sauces can be served with the vegetables–try the tikka sauce on page 78, with or without the addition of yogurt, or simply crème fraîche or yogurt seasoned with lemon or lime and any herb you fancy. You could also add a couple of spoonfuls of wine or brandy to the roasting vegetables and make them quite grand. A few slivers of wild or cultivated mushrooms can also greatly enhance the flavor.

SERVES
4 – 6

INGREDIENTS

- 4 medium carrots, cut into ¾ in chunks
- 4 medium parsnips, cut into ¾ in chunks
- ½ lb shallots or baby onions, peeled and left whole
- 3 medium potatoes, peeled or unpeeled, and cut into wedges
- 4 leeks, cut into 2 in lengths
- 1 lb pumpkin, cut into 1¼ in chunks
- 1½ cups mushrooms
- 6 garlic cloves, left whole
- 5 tbsp olive oil
- 1 tbsp mixed chopped herbs, such as thyme, rosemary, and parsley
- 1 tbsp tamari
- pinch of soft brown sugar
- salt and freshly ground black pepper

METHOD

Preheat the oven to its highest setting. Mix all the vegetables together with the unpeeled garlic, oil, herbs, tamari, sugar, and salt and pepper, and place in a large ovenproof dish or sheet. Place in the oven and roast for 35–40 minutes or until all the vegetables are tender.

salads

Cranks has always maintained a reputation for its salads: Huge bowls of fresh and colorful raw ingredients with interesting dressings and toppings. There is such an abundance of weird and wonderful produce available in shops and markets that *the art of salad making is now more interesting and exciting than ever.*

Salads succeed best when served as a course in their own right. They can be composed of cooked ingredients and eaten warm, or dressed with an infinite variety of croûtons and seeds, slivers of dried fruit, or parings of strong cheese. Try them served with nothing but extra virgin olive oil and vinegar, or dressed extravagantly with thick luxuriant sauces, creamy with blue cheese or biting with garlic and chili peppers. Nuts may be toasted and tossed in. Harder vegetables can be grated and left to marinate in thick, rich dressings, while delicate leaves require the thinnest of coatings just before serving.

SALADE CUITE (CHOUCHOUKA)

I have eaten my mother's salade cuite all my life and this is what we have always called it. It was only in writing the recipe for this book that my father recalled that it is in fact the Chouchouka of Algerian origin. The original is cooked slowly and for a long time and turned almost into a confit. I cook this recipe for far less time, which gives a much lighter result, but try it out both ways. In either case, do not skimp on the garlic.

SERVES

6

INGREDIENTS

- 1 red, 1 green, and 1 yellow bell pepper
- ¼ cup olive oil
- 1 lb ripe tomatoes, cut into quarters
- dash of Tabasco or cayenne pepper
- 5 garlic cloves, chopped

METHOD

Put the peppers under a hot broiler until the skins are charred, turning at least once to char evenly. Put in a bowl and cover with a plate until cool enough to handle (this makes them easier to peel). Peel, deseed, and cut into strips when they are cool enough to handle.

Heat the oil in a skillet and add the chopped tomatoes. Sauté for 4–5 minutes until broken down into a sauce. Add the Tabasco or cayenne pepper and the chopped garlic. Sauté for a further 2–3 minutes, stirring regularly, then add the pepper strips and continue to cook for 3–4 minutes or, for a more authentic result, 10–12 minutes so that practically all the juice is evaporated and you are left with a thick sauce. Eat at room temperature as part of an antipasto, served with several other simple salads and chunks of warm bread of any nationality.

FENNEL AND TOMATO SALAD

This is a refreshing and clean-tasting salad. The fennel handles the much stronger flavors of garlic and olives surprisingly well. This salad works equally well served straightaway, or you can let it marinate for an hour or so.

SERVES
4 – 6

INGREDIENTS

- 6 small, perfect young fennel bulbs
- 3 garlic cloves, sliced paper thin
- 5 tbsp olive oil
- 3 tbsp balsamic vinegar

- 1 lb ripe plum tomatoes
- 1¼ cups Provençal black olives
- 2 oz fresh Parmesan cheese, cut into thin slivers
- salt and freshly ground black pepper

METHOD

Trim the fronds and ends from the fennel bulbs. Slice thinly along the vertical grain. Either leave as is or cut the slices into thin strips. Mix the finely sliced garlic, oil, vinegar, and salt and pepper, and pour over the fennel. Allow to marinate for 20 minutes or so. Then add the tomatoes cut into wedges, and finally the black olives and the Parmesan.

ROAST FENNEL, BELGIAN ENDIVE, AND ARTICHOKE SALAD

WITH FRESH GARLIC, PINE NUTS, AND SUNDRIED TOMATO DRESSING

There are sweet and bittersweet flavors in this roasted and broiled vegetable salad, and the younger and fresher the vegetables the better.

SERVES

2

INGREDIENTS

- 4 small, young fennel bulbs
- 3 heads chicory, red or white
- 1 cup canned artichoke hearts, cut in half, or 12 baby artichokes, hearts and stems only
- 2 fresh garlic bulbs, outer skin removed and each cut into 6

- 5–6 tbsp olive oil
- 1 tbsp very red sundried tomato paste
- 1 cup herbed green olives
- 1 tbsp pine nuts, toasted
- bunch of cilantro, chopped
- sea salt and freshly ground black pepper

METHOD

Preheat the oven to 475°F. Trim the fennel and cut lengthwise into 6 pieces. Trim the Belgian endive, removing any old leaves, and cut lengthwise into 6. Cut the artichoke hearts in half.

Mix all the vegetables together with the garlic, olive oil, and some sea salt and freshly ground black pepper. Place in an ovenproof dish. Bake in the preheated oven for 15 minutes, and then place under a hot broiler for 5–6 minutes to brown.

Remove from the heat, stir well, and transfer to a large colorful plate. Just before serving, dot the sundried tomato paste all over, as well as the green olives, the toasted pine nuts, and fresh cilantro, and mix. Serve warm or at room temperature.

PANZANELLA

This traditional Tuscan salad makes use of stale bread. Any crusty white bread will do, though if you have some, an Italian ciabatta is most appropriate. Use a peppery Tuscan olive oil, and make this in the summer when ripe vine tomatoes are plentiful. Because of the simplicity of the ingredients used, it is even more important than usual that they are of the best possible quality.

SERVES

6

INGREDIENTS

- 2 stale ciabatta loaves, sliced
- 2 lb fresh plum tomatoes
- 4–6 garlic cloves, crushed to a paste with a little olive oil and sea salt
- 1½ cups Tuscan olive oil, plus extra for serving
- 5 tbsp balsamic vinegar
- 3 red bell peppers
- 3 yellow bell peppers
- 2 fresh red chili peppers
- ½ cup capers in salt, large fresh ones if possible
- 1½ cups herbed black olives
- large bunch of basil
- sea salt and freshly ground black pepper

METHOD

Place the bread in a large bowl. Skin the tomatoes with a vegetable peeler and then cut them in half. Place a strainer over a bowl. Hold the tomato halves over the strainer and scoop out the seeds, allowing the juices to drip through. Set the tomato halves aside. Season the tomato juice with the garlic and some pepper, adding most of the olive oil and balsamic vinegar. Pour this dressing over the bread and toss until it is all absorbed, adding more olive oil if necessary.

Broil the peppers and chili peppers until charred on all sides (see page 173), then cut peppers into 8 strips and the chili peppers very finely. Rinse the salt off the capers.

Place some of the soaked bread in a dish, then add some of the other ingredients, then more bread and continue in this fashion until all the ingredients are used up but with the final layer made up of the colorful vegetables. Allow to rest at room temperature for an hour and serve with more olive oil.

BROILED BABY VEGETABLES

MARINATED IN CHILI PEPPER OIL AND BALSAMIC VINEGAR

These vegetables are so charming you could give them as a gift, layered according to type in an old-fashioned preserving jar. Keep them refrigerated and eat within 3–4 days. Olive oil is just as desirable if you cannot find chili pepper oil. Serve on warmed focaccia or ciabatta bread, with a slice of goat's cheese, a few olives, and a small mound of perfect arugula.

SERVES 4 – 6

INGREDIENTS

- ½ lb baby zucchini, gently scored with a sharp knife
- ½ cup sundried tomatoes in oil
- ½ lb baby eggplant
- ½ lb firm but red and ripe tomatoes, cut in half
- ½ cup chili pepper oil
- ½ cup balsamic vinegar
- 2 garlic cloves, chopped
- I piece chili pepper, finely diced
- juice of ½ lime
- sea salt and freshly ground black pepper

METHOD

Wash the vegetables and baste with half the chili pepper oil and some sea salt. Place under a hot broiler for 3–4 minutes, turning over until they are charred on all sides. Remove from the heat. Mix the balsamic vinegar, chopped garlic, chili pepper, lime juice, salt, and pepper, and baste all the vegetables.

Thoroughly wash a preserving jar and rinse it out with boiling water. Dry carefully, then add first a layer of zucchini, then one of sundried tomatoes, then one of eggplant, then a second of sundried tomatoes. Complete with a layer of broiled tomatoes, sprinkled with fresh sea salt and the remaining oil. Seal and refrigerate. Return to room temperature before serving.

CHICKPEA SALAD

WITH CILANTRO, PAPRIKA, CUMIN, AND YOGURT SAUCE

This is a particularly rich and full-flavored salad which can form the main course of a cold summer lunch.

INGREDIENTS

- 4 cups cooked chickpeas
- 1 cup onions, diced
- 2 scallions, neatly chopped
- ¼ cup parsley, finely chopped
- ¼ cup cilantro, finely chopped
- 1 tbsp paprika
- 1 tbsp cumin
- 2 garlic cloves, finely chopped
- scant juice of ½ lemon

- 1 cup olive oil
- 3 tbsp tamari
- 1 lb baby spinach
- salt and freshly ground black pepper

FOR THE SAUCE

- 2 cups plain or Greek yogurt
- ¼ cup cilantro, chopped
- 1 garlic clove, finely chopped

METHOD

Mix together all the ingredients, except the spinach, 3 tbsp of the olive oil, and 1 tbsp of the tamari, and allow to marinate for several hours. The salad should look rich and red, the olive oil brilliant with paprika. At the last moment, toss the baby spinach with the reserved oil and tamari, as well as a few squeezes of lemon juice, in another bowl. Mix the sauce ingredients together.

Heap the spinach loosely onto a plate and spoon the chickpea salad on top with the yogurt sauce served separately.

NEW POTATO AND GREEN BEAN SALAD

WITH RED ONION AND CHEDDAR CHEESE

Simple to prepare, this salad is a complete summer meal in itself. Use the smallest new potatoes available so you can leave them whole. As is often the case, this salad is better when left to sit for a while to allow the potatoes to absorb the dressing ingredients. The green beans, however, should be tossed in at the last minute to avoid being discolored by the balsamic vinegar.

SERVES

6

INGREDIENTS

- 1 lb small new potatoes
- ½ lb green beans, trimmed
- ½ cup red onions, sliced
- 1 cup black olives
- 3–4 pieces sundried tomatoes in oil, cut into thin slivers
- 5 oz Cheddar cheese, cut into cubes

FOR THE DRESSING

- 1 tbsp grain mustard
- ½ cup olive oil
- 1 tbsp balsamic vinegar
- 1 garlic clove, crushed
- salt and freshly ground black pepper

METHOD

Place the potatoes in a pan of salted boiling water and boil for about 14 minutes or until the potatoes are tender. Bring another pan of salted water to a boil and blanch the green beans for 2–3 minutes, then drain, and refresh under cold water.

Place the warm potatoes in a bowl and add the sliced red onion, olives, and sundried tomato slivers. Finally, mix all the dressing ingredients in a small bowl, season, and add to the potato salad. Toss in the green beans and Cheddar just before serving.

BEAN SPROUTS AND SEED SALAD

WITH GARLIC AND BEAN CURD MAYONNAISE

You might expect to find a salad of this ilk in a health food manual, but if you can put your prejudices aside, you will find that as well as being supremely nutritious, it is also extremely delicious. The bean curd mayonnaise is more than you will need but it is so delicious that you should make a large batch while you're at it (it will keep for a few days in the fridge), or simply make only half the recipe if you intend to use it for this salad alone.

INGREDIENTS

- ¼ cup pumpkin seeds
- 4 cups bean sprouts, a mixture of mung and lentil
- 2 scallions, finely sliced
- ½ avocado, cut into cubes
- I carrot, cut into thin rings (optional)
- I sheet nori seaweed
- I level tbsp nori flakes
- large handful of fresh cilantro, leaves taken off the stalks

FOR THE DRESSING

- 6 oz bean curd
- ¼ cup olive oil
- ¾ cup water
- I tbsp tamari
- I tsp Tabasco
- 2 garlic cloves, crushed
- juice of ½ lime
- salt and freshly ground black pepper

METHOD

Dry-roast the pumpkin seeds in a pan set over a high heat with a little added salt but no oil.

Mix together all the salad ingredients except the seaweed, nori flakes, and cilantro, and set aside. Blend the dressing ingredients until absolutely smooth. Add half of the dressing to the salad and mix well. Place a sheet of seaweed onto a plate, pile on the salad in a mound, and garnish with the nori flakes and the cilantro.

MIXED BEAN SALAD
WITH CILANTRO SAUCE AND BROILED
RED BELL PEPPER

The association of beans and bean sprouts with vegetarian food has not always been a happy one, but this colorful and delicious salad should change a few minds. Canned kidney beans are perfect with their glistening skins, but I prefer to cook my own chickpeas and navy beans.

INGREDIENTS

SERVES

6

- 1½ cups cooked kidney beans
- 1½ cups cooked navy beans
- 1½ cups cooked chickpeas
- ½ lb green beans, cleaned
- 1 red bell pepper, broiled, skinned, and cut into slivers (see page 173)
- small handful fresh cilantro leaves
- 1 red onion, finely chopped

FOR THE DRESSING
- ¼ cup heavy cream
- 1 tbsp mayonnaise
- juice of ½ lemon
- 4 tbsp coconut milk
- 2 garlic cloves, crushed
- salt and freshly ground black pepper

METHOD

(If you are using dried beans, soak them overnight, keeping each kind separate. The next day, drain them, place in a saucepan, cover with cold water, add 1 bay leaf and 1 garlic clove, peeled and halved. Bring to a boil, then reduce the heat and simmer for 1½ hours, until the beans are tender. Drain.) Put the cooked kidney beans, navy beans and chickpeas in a bowl and set aside.

Cook the green beans in a pan of salted boiling water until just tender but still slightly firm. Immediately refresh under cold water and set aside.

Make the dressing by mixing the cream, mayonnaise, lemon juice, and coconut milk until well amalgamated. Add the crushed garlic and season with salt and pepper. Mix in with the beans and chickpeas until well coated. Allow to sit for a few minutes before mixing in the green beans until well coated and, at the final moment, the red bell pepper slivers, the fresh cilantro, and the chopped red onion. Serve warm or cold.

ARUGULA SALAD

WITH PARMESAN AND ASPARAGUS

This is the kind of salad that is perfect as an easy appetizer or can replace a vegetable dish for a summer meal. I love asparagus: White or green, thick-stemmed or thin, English or otherwise, in season or not. Arugula sown in spring grows profusely all summer long, making the small overpriced supermarket packets looks ridiculous. It has a more peppery taste and, by growing it yourself, you can afford to pile it onto plates in generous mounds. All bitter leaves are served well by mustard, especially grain, which is a natural companion for the asparagus too.

SERVES

6

INGREDIENTS

- 1 lb asparagus, trimmed
- 6 tbsp olive oil
- 1 tsp grain mustard
- 1 scant tbsp balsamic vinegar
- 1 garlic clove, crushed
- ½ arugula
- ¼ lb fresh Parmesan cheese
- salt and freshly ground black pepper

METHOD

Peel the stems of the asparagus, if necessary. Bring a pan of salted water to a boil and blanch the asparagus for 1–2 minutes, depending on their size. Meanwhile, quickly combine the oil, mustard, balsamic vinegar, crushed garlic, and salt and pepper. Immediately pour over the warm asparagus and toss into the arugula. Top with fine shavings of fresh Parmesan and serve at once.

AVOCADO WITH MIXED LEAVES AND PESTO

Another simple, rich salad which makes a delicious appetizer served with chunks of flat oily Arabic bread or focaccia. Hass avocados are invariably the best, with rich texture, but you should still always buy one more than you need because it's practically impossible to guarantee that you won't land on one with blackened flesh.

SERVES
4 – 6

INGREDIENTS

- 2 avocados, peeled and cut into even-sized 1 in chunks
- ½ lb mixed lettuce leaves, preferably very young

FOR THE DRESSING

- ¼ cup good quality pesto
- ¼ cup olive oil
- salt and freshly ground black pepper

METHOD

Mix the dressing ingredients together and then toss with the avocado. Mix with the lettuce leaves and serve at once.

BELGIAN ENDIVE, WATERCRESS, AND POMEGRANATE SALAD
WITH WALNUT OIL

The pomegranate seeds in this salad look like jewels. Pick a pomegranate with bright, smooth, deeply colored skin. Pomegranate and sesame seeds are used to herald in the Jewish New Year and are symbols of bounty and fecundity. Squeezing juice from a pomegranate is messy but fun!

SERVES
4 – 6

INGREDIENTS

- 1 pomegranate
- ⅓ lb watercress
- 2 heads Belgian endive, outer leaves removed and chopped

- 1 tbsp walnut oil
- 1 tbsp sesame seeds, lightly toasted
- freshly ground black pepper

METHOD

Cut off a third from the pomegranate and set aside. Remove the seeds from the remaining two-thirds. Mix the seeds together with the watercress and Belgian endive. Then squeeze the juice from the remaining pomegranate into the walnut oil and mix. Pour all over the salad, sprinkle with freshly ground black pepper and sesame seeds, and serve at once.

NEW POTATO SALAD

WITH HERBS AND PARMESAN

Potato salads are invariably best served warm, so the dressing is more readily absorbed. But forget stodgy potato mayonnaise and try an olive oil dressing, rich with fresh herbs, garlic, and Parmesan instead. The salad can form a base for other ingredients such as spinach or arugula, which will wilt in the heat, or a few wild mushrooms, cut into slivers, sautéed briefly, and thrown in. Potatoes love onion, so very finely chopped, almost minced, red onion will go beautifully. Green beans are another successful addition. The Parmesan can be replaced by another strong-tasting cheese, such as pecorino.

SERVES

6

INGREDIENTS

- 2 lb new potatoes, cut in half if large
- 1–2 garlic cloves, crushed
- 5 fl oz olive oil
- 1 bunch of chives, finely snipped
- 1 tsp fresh thyme or other herb of your choice, chopped

- 1 tsp fresh chervil or basil, chopped
- ¼ lb Parmesan cheese, thinly shaved
- sea salt crystals and freshly ground black pepper

METHOD

Place the potatoes in a large pan of salted water and bring to a boil. Cook for 10–15 minutes or until the potatoes are tender. Drain and set aside. Meanwhile, mix the finely crushed garlic with the olive oil and salt and pepper. Mix this and the fresh herbs with the potatoes while they are still warm and finally, just before serving, top with the shavings of Parmesan.

KOHLRABI AND PEAR
WITH DOLCELATTE (ITALIAN BLUE CHEESE)
DRESSING AND FRESH WALNUTS

This is an unusual salad which requires pears at the very peak of perfection. William pears are the best, especially when their skins are lightly tinged with orange. I use dolcelatte, the Italian blue cheese, because it is the mildest and creamiest of blue cheeses and goes beautifully with walnuts. Use wet, fresh walnuts when they are available at the start of their season in early fall, but whatever you do, don't use those rancid-tasting and often bitter pre-packed walnuts.

SERVES

6

INGREDIENTS

- 2 kohlrabi, peeled and sliced practically paper-thin
- I avocado, peeled and cut into thin slices
- 4 perfect William pears, cored and sliced into thin segments
- 3 walnuts, shelled and roughly chopped

FOR THE DRESSING

- ¼ lb dolcelatte (Italian blue cheese)
- ¾ cup sour cream
- I–2 tbsp warm water
- freshly ground black pepper

METHOD

Bring a pan of salted water to a boil and plunge the slices of kohlrabi into it for 10 seconds. Drain thoroughly.

Assemble the salad, arranging the ingredients in concentric rings, starting with kohlrabi slices, then avocado slices, and finishing off with pear slices.

To make the dressing, blend the dolcelatte with the sour cream and warm water to make a dressing that pours easily. Drizzle all over the salad and complete by scattering the chopped walnuts and freshly ground black pepper over and around the salad.

CHERRY TOMATOES, OLIVES, BABY CUCUMBER, AND BABY MOZZARELLA

A dead easy salad which looks dead good! Baby cucumbers are much sweeter than the larger varieties. If you want to make this in advance, add the cucumbers only at the last minute.

INGREDIENTS

- 5 fl oz olive oil
- 1 tbsp balsamic vinegar
- 1 garlic clove, crushed
- 5 oz baby mozzarella cheeses or 1 large ball cut into chunks
- 1 lb cherry tomatoes
- handful fresh basil leaves, purple or green
- 3 tbsp sundried tomatoes in oil, finely sliced
- 1 cup mixed green and black herb olives
- ½ lb baby cucumber (about 3), peeled and cut into ½ in chunks
- salt and freshly ground black pepper

METHOD

Mix the olive oil with the balsamic vinegar, garlic, and salt and pepper, and then marinate the mozzarella for 10 minutes. Mix with the cherry tomatoes, basil, sundried tomatoes, olives, and chopped cucumber, and serve with warm bread.

BEET SALAD

WITH RED ONION AND BALSAMIC VINEGAR

Three strong flavors for a simple, beautifully red salad. I know someone who went on a beet fast for several weeks. It's not what I recommend you do, but on this salad I'd be tempted.

SERVES

6

INGREDIENTS

- 1½ lb cooked beets
- 1 tbsp almond or corn oil
- 1 tsp grain mustard
- ½ cup balsamic vinegar
- dash of Tabasco
- 1 tsp caraway seeds, pounded with a little oil in a mortar and pestle

- 1 small bunch flat leaf parsley or cilantro, coarsely chopped
- 2 red onions, diced very small
- 3 oz feta cheese
- coarse sea salt and freshly ground black pepper

METHOD

Cut the beets into slices ⅛ in thick or into ½ in dice. Mix the oil, mustard, vinegar, Tabasco, and caraway seeds into a thin dressing. Pour over the beets and set aside for at least half an hour to allow the flavors to mingle and develop.

Just before serving, mix in the fresh parsley or cilantro (reserving a little for the garnish), the red onion, and finally the coarse sea salt. Pour out onto a plate and crumble the feta cheese all over the top. Finish off with the remaining herbs and a little coarsely ground black pepper.

BROILED EGGPLANT

WITH SMOKED MOZZARELLA FRITTERS
AND TOMATOES

Jenny Wright, who used to work at Cranks, mentioned the combination of eggplant and smoked mozzarella to me, and I could not get it out of my mind until I made this recipe. You will probably have to order the smoked mozzarella from a specialty cheese store, although Italian delicatessens often stock it.

INGREDIENTS

- 2 medium eggplant, cut into ¼ in slices
- 6 tbsp olive oil
- 1 lb good firm, bright red tomatoes
- several leaves basil, finely shredded, plus extra for garnish
- 1½ cups toasted fine bread crumbs
- 3 eggs, medium sized, beaten
- 1 quart corn oil, for deep-frying

- 6 oz smoked mozzarella cheese, cut into ¼ in slices
- ½ lb arugula

FOR THE DRESSING

- 1 heaping tbsp grain mustard
- 3 tbsp balsamic vinegar
- 5 fl oz olive oil
- freshly ground black pepper

METHOD

Brush the eggplant slices with olive oil on one side and place under a hot broiler for 5 minutes. Turn over, brush the other side with olive oil, and repeat. Let cool slightly, then cut into strips and set aside. Slice the tomatoes and set aside. Make the dressing by whisking the mustard with the vinegar and adding the olive oil and pepper.

Mix the shredded basil and bread crumbs in a shallow dish. Put the eggs in another shallow dish. Heat the corn oil until very hot and then turn the heat down. Dip the mozzarella slices in the beaten egg and then in the bread crumbs. Drop gently into the hot oil and turn over quickly to lightly brown both sides; about 20–30 seconds. Remove with a slotted spoon and place on a plate lined with paper towels.

To serve, pile a mound of arugula onto each plate, add tomato slices all the way round. Place the fried mozzarella on top, and scatter generously with the strips of fried eggplant. Drizzle the dressing all over. Serve immediately, garnished with a few small basil leaves.

CHINESE LEAF SALAD

WITH WALNUTS AND
CHEESE IN LIGHT MAYONNAISE

This combination of ingredients is irresistible and rather like a sophisticated version of coleslaw. Serve it straightaway and don't let it sit around or it will lose all its appealing crunch.

SERVES
4 – 6

INGREDIENTS

- 1 head of Chinese leaf
- 4 oz mature Cheddar cheese, cut into cubes
- ½ cup walnuts, shelled
- ½ cup yogurt

- ½ cup mayonnaise
- ¼ lb watercress
- salt and freshly ground black pepper

METHOD

Remove the outer leaves of the Chinese leaf and discard. Chop the rest and mix with the Cheddar and walnuts. Mix the yogurt and mayonnaise, and pour over the Chinese leaf, Cheddar, and walnuts. Serve on a bed of watercress, sprinkled with black pepper.

WARM MUSHROOM SALAD
WITH QUAILS' EGGS

A warm salad of wild mushrooms cooked for the briefest
time, and quails' eggs with yolks still soft in the middle. Work
carefully to remove the fine shells, using a small sharp knife
to cut through the shell and inner membrane. If you are
making this as an appetizer for a dinner party, serve it on
tender, young frisée leaves.

INGREDIENTS

SERVES

6

- 18–24 quails' eggs
- 5 tbsp olive oil
- 2 lb mixed wild mushrooms
- 2 garlic cloves, finely chopped

- 1 tbsp brandy
- 1 tsp tamari
- 1 tbsp finely chopped basil
- salt and freshly ground black pepper

METHOD

To cook the quails' eggs, boil for $2^1/_2$ minutes, and then plunge them into cold water.
Cut one egg open to check that it is cooked. Peel immediately under cold, running
water, and set aside.

Heat the oil gently in a skillet and sauté the mushrooms with the garlic, brandy,
tamari, and salt and pepper for 3–4 minutes. Transfer to a plate and arrange the quails'
eggs, cut in half, over the top. Garnish with the finely chopped basil and serve.

WARM PASTA SALAD

WITH ARUGULA, BLACK OLIVES
AND SUNDRIED TOMATOES

Warm pasta salads are delicious when eaten more or less as soon as they have been made. Add a few Parmesan shavings to each serving and a small mound of perfect arugula leaves for a salad that is as pretty as it is delicious. I leave the shape of the pasta to you and the ingenuity of modern pasta manufacturers.

SERVES

6

INGREDIENTS

- ½ cup olive oil or oil that the tomatoes have been marinating in
- 1 lb pasta shapes
- 2–3 garlic cloves, crushed to a paste with a little sea salt
- 1 tbsp balsamic vinegar (optional)
- dash of Tabasco
- 1 cup Provençal black olives
- ½ cup sundried tomatoes in oil, cut in slivers
- ½ cup toasted pine nuts
- 1 large bunch basil, leaves only
- ⅓ lb arugula
- 2 oz fresh Parmesan cheese
- salt and freshly ground black pepper

METHOD

Bring a large pan of salted water to a boil. Add a spoonful of olive oil and the pasta. Cook according to package instructions. Drain, and run briefly under cold water to prevent the pasta from sticking together.

Meanwhile, mix the remaining olive oil with the garlic paste, balsamic vinegar, Tabasco, and salt and pepper to taste. Pour over the warm pasta and mix with the olives, sundried tomatoes, pine nuts, basil, and half the arugula so that it just begins to wilt in the remaining warmth. Use the rest of the arugula to pile into light and pretty mounds on top of the pasta. Finish off with several shavings of Parmesan.

CAULIFLOWER AND BROCCOLI SALAD

WITH BROILED RED BELL PEPPERS AND GRAIN MUSTARD DRESSING

This dressing can be as bold as you dare, but save it for the weekend or drastically reduce the garlic count! The longer you can allow the cauliflower to marinate in the garlic dressing, the better. I rarely resist the temptation to add olives to this salad, but then I rarely resist the temptation to add olives to anything, so they are not included in the ingredients but are left up to you. Cauliflower can take quantities of grain mustard, so add as much as you wish.

SERVES

6

INGREDIENTS

- 1 large cauliflower, outer leaves and stalk removed, and separated into flowerets
- 1 lb broccoli, separated into flowerets
- 2 red bell peppers, charbroiled, peeled, and thinly sliced (see page 173)

FOR THE DRESSING

- ½ cup extra-virgin olive oil
- 1 heaping tbsp grain mustard
- 3 tbsp fresh tarragon, picked off the stalks
- 4 garlic cloves, finely crushed
- dash of Tabasco
- dash of balsamic vinegar
- salt and freshly ground black pepper

METHOD

Plunge the cauliflower and broccoli flowerets into a pan of salted boiling water and blanch for 1 minute until tender but still firm. Meanwhile, combine the dressing ingredients. Place the cauliflower and broccoli in a bowl with the red bell pepppers and pour over the dressing while the cauliflower and broccoli are still hot. Add more grain mustard to taste if necessary. Add olives if using, and serve with a simple couscous salad or warm pasta bows, or as part of a combined salad plate.

desserts

There are some people who feel that a meal isn't complete without a proper dessert, with lashings of cream or, at the very least, a light, fruity dessert. In this chapter, you'll find something to suit you, whatever your preference.

Over the years, both classic and contemporary desserts have been incorporated into the Cranks menu, in recognition of the fact that ordinary human beings are really quite content to follow salad with a proper dessert. Perhaps the day will come when the human race will wonder at its sugar consumption as it becomes, en masse, satisfied with super-healthy, sugar-free foods, but I doubt it. However, just in case, in this chapter I have included some rather delicious fruit-based desserts for you to try.

Several traditional British desserts, such as bread and butter pudding, are also featured—fondness for these certainly never seems to wane—as well as some rather elegant pâtisseries that are worthy of the smartest of restaurants. So turn the pages and take your pick from baked winter fruit, crème brûlée, chocolate roulade, fruit savarin, sticky date pudding ...

ALMOND MERINGUE

WITH CHOCOLATE MOUSSE AND CHANTILLY

This recipe is inspired by one that has been in my family for generations. Originally layered with sponge cake and buttercream, as well as the meringue, chocolate mousse, and Chantilly, it was referred to as a traditional Russian wedding cake. Its origins are quite obviously French though, and a delicious version, known as progrès, is sold in Parisian pâtisseries. As it is, this dessert is unbelievably grand and decadent. I give a generous recipe because you'll only want to make it for a special occasion.

To achieve perfect results, set the oven temperature very low, so that the meringues cook slowly and stay white. Use the best quality wax paper, and oil very lightly with a little corn or almond oil. Respect the rules of using a sparklingly clean bowl with no trace of greasiness, and be sure to avoid getting even the slightest drop of egg yolk into the whites. Finally, resist adding more sugar to the meringue until the previous amount is well incorporated or you will end up with a gooey mess which does not peel off the paper.

INGREDIENTS

SERVES 10–12

- 8 egg whites, medium sized, at room temperature
- 2 cups sugar, mixed with ½ tsp cornstarch
- 1 cup toasted whole almonds, coarsely chopped

FOR THE CHANTILLY

- 1 cup heavy cream
- 1 tbsp confectioners' sugar

CHOCOLATE MOUSSE

- 1 cup heavy cream, chilled
- 1 tbsp confectioners' sugar
- 1 cup butter, lightly softened
- 1 cup unsweetened cocoa
- ½ cup plus 2 tbsp sugar
- 6 egg yolks, medium sized
- 3 tbsp brandy

METHOD

Preheat the oven to 250°F.

To make the meringue, place the egg whites in a large, clean mixer bowl. Measure the sugar and have it easily at hand. Draw a circle 8 in in diameter, using an upturned plate or cake pan as a guide, on 3 separate pieces of wax paper. Cut out, lightly brush with oil, and set aside.

Begin by whisking the egg whites at a gentle speed so they break down completely, and then turn to the fastest speed until they stand in stiff peaks. Immediately add 1 tbsp of the sugar until it is thoroughly whisked in and then slowly, and spoon by spoon, add the rest of the sugar, mixed with the cornstarch. It is essential that each spoonful is well incorporated before you add another. I count 10 seconds between each spoonful.

Cover one circle of paper with a third of this plain meringue, using a tablespoon to lift the mixture onto the paper, and then lightly swirl around with a clean skewer or the tines of a fork. Add the coarsely chopped nuts to the remaining meringue mixture and divide between the other two pieces of paper, spreading evenly and swirling as before. Place in the preheated (albeit very low) oven and allow it to dry out for 1 hour. Remove from oven. Turn each meringue upside down onto a large flat plate and carefully peel off the paper.

While the meringue is in the oven, make the chocolate mousse. Whisk the cream, adding the confectioners' sugar until it just holds stiff peaks. Set aside. Place the softened butter, unsweetened cocoa, and sugar in a large mixer bowl. Add the egg yolks and brandy, and whisk, slowly at first, as otherwise the unsweetened cocoa will rise in a cloud. When mixed in, increase the speed, and continue to whisk for several minutes until the mixture is smooth and voluminous and there is no trace of powderiness. Fold in the sweetened whipped cream and set aside.

Make the Chantilly by whisking the cream and sugar together.

To assemble, place one circle of almond meringue, smooth side up, on a large flat serving plate. Spread carefully with half the chocolate mousse, taking the mixture up to the edges but thinly enough so that it does not spill out when you add the next layer. Then cover with the layer of plain meringue, the remaining chocolate mousse, the Chantilly on top of that, and finally the second almond meringue. Serve at once.

(Both the meringue and chocolate mousse freeze very well. The chocolate mousse will have to be thawed out first, but the meringue can be used straight from the freezer. Alternatively, freeze the assembled dessert and eat it while it is still very cold.)

COCONUT, CARDAMOM, AND LIME ICE CREAM

You could substitute ordinary milk for the coconut milk and replace the cardamom seeds with a vanilla pod to make a simpler ice cream if you wish. Either way, this ice cream is excellent served with the Pumpkin Pie on page 251.

SERVES

6

INGREDIENTS

- 1¼ cups coconut milk
- 1¼ cups heavy cream
- zest of 1 lime

- ½ tsp cardamom seeds, crushed
- 1 cup sugar
- 6 egg yolks

METHOD

Place the coconut milk, heavy cream, lime zest, cardamom seeds, and half the sugar in a saucepan and bring to a boil, then immediately remove from heat. Cream the egg yolks with the remaining sugar in a separate bowl, then pour the hot mixture into them, stirring all the time. Return this mixture to the pan and heat over very low heat, stirring constantly with a wooden spoon, until the custard is thick enough to coat the back of the spoon. The custard must on no account be allowed to boil.

Strain the custard through a fine strainer and set aside to cool. Finally, pour the cooled mixture into a plastic bowl and put in the freezer.

About 30 minutes later, when the ice cream is beginning to set, remove from the freezer and beat thoroughly with an electric hand whisk to break down any ice crystals that may have formed. Repeat this process two or three times until the ice cream is completely set. The whole freezing process takes 2–3 hours.

EXOTIC FRUIT SALAD IN RASPBERRY SAUCE

SERVED IN A CHOCOLATE BOWL

This is the queen of fruit salads. The raspberry sauce should be thick and as bright as possible, with all the tiny seeds strained out. Use this or another combination of fresh fruit.

SERVES
8

INGREDIENTS

- 3 or 4 ripe but still firm apricots
- 2 ripe but still firm nectarines
- I ripe mango
- I ripe papaya or pawpaw
- I charentais or other melon
- 3 ripe passion fruit
- ½ cup bright red strawberries
- ½ cup blueberries or blackberries
- ½ cup Chinese gooseberries
- ½ cup black cherries

FOR THE CHOCOLATE BOWL

- 8 oz (8 squares) good quality unsweetened dark chocolate
- I tbsp almond or corn oil

FOR THE SAUCE

- I cup frozen raspberries, blended and strained
- ¼ cup sugar

TO SERVE

- 2 cups heavy cream or crème fraîche

METHOD

To make the chocolate bowl, break the chocolate into pieces and place in a bowl set over a pan of boiling water until melted. Line a 10 in plastic bowl with foil, pressing it down firmly all the way round. Very lightly brush with the almond or corn oil. Use a pastry brush to paint a layer of chocolate onto the foil, making sure it is well covered. Freeze until set and repeat twice more until all the chocolate is used up.

For the fruit salad, carefully wash all the fruit. Remove all seeds and pits from the apricots, nectarines, mango, and papaya. Cut into neat 1 in squares or use a melon baller on the melon and papaya. Scoop out the seeds from the passion fruit and slice the strawberries if they are large. Mix all the fruit together.

To make the raspberry sauce, place the raspberries and sugar in a blender and blend until smooth. Pass through a fine strainer to remove all the seeds: This is essential. Mix into the fruit salad. Just before serving, ease the foil-covered chocolate bowl from the plastic bowl and carefully peel off the foil. Place the chocolate bowl on a large serving plate and fill with fruit salad. Serve with whipped heavy cream or crème fraîche.

LEMON TART

This is a particularly lemony and creamy version of a popular and classic dessert. Another version can be made with orange or lime juice instead of lemon, and the addition of coconut to infuse in the cream.

INGREDIENTS

FOR THE TART SHELL

- ½ cup plus 2 tbsp unsalted butter, cut into small pieces
- 2 tbsp sugar
- 2 cups all purpose flour, sifted
- ice-cold water

FOR THE FILLING

- 1¼ cups heavy cream
- zest and juice of 5 lemons
- 4–5 cardamon pods, split open (optional)
- 1¼ cups sugar
- 9 eggs, medium sized
- 1 tsp confectioners' sugar to garnish

METHOD

For the filling, heat the cream with the lemon zest and cardamom pods, if using, to just boiling point, then remove from the heat and leave to infuse for several hours or preferably overnight. Then strain, add the sugar and lemon juice, and beat in the eggs one at a time.

Make the tart shell by placing the butter, sugar, and flour in a bowl and working lightly with your fingers until the mixture turns to fine crumbs. Bring the dough together by adding a little ice-cold water. Set aside in the fridge for about 20 minutes.

Preheat the oven to 400°F. Roll out the dough and line an 11 in round, loose-bottomed tart pan, reserving a small amount of dough to patch up any cracks which may appear after it has been first baked. Prick all over with a fork and bake in the preheated oven for 15 minutes or until pale gold.

Let the tart shell cool, then pour in the lemon custard, and bake for 1–1½ hours at 250°F. Do not allow the top to brown at all. When just set, remove from the oven and let cool for a couple of hours. Lightly dust with confectioners' sugar around the edges and serve.

CREME BRULEE

These individual desserts are easy to make, and look stunning with their topping of caramelized sugar. To put the leftover vanilla pod to good use, wipe it clean and leave it to dry out after infusing the milk, then put it in an airtight jar with some sugar—you will then have vanilla sugar to use as you would ordinary sugar, but with a lovely, delicate vanilla scent.

SERVES

8

INGREDIENTS

- 1½ cups soft brown sugar
- 12–13 egg yolks, medium sized

- 2½ cups heavy cream
- 1 vanilla pod

METHOD

Preheat the oven to 350°F.

Mix half the sugar with the egg yolks in an electric mixer at low speed, until thick and creamy. Gently heat the heavy cream with the vanilla pod, but do not boil. Cover the pan and let stand for 30 minutes. Remove the vanilla pod. With the mixer turned even lower, gradually add the cream to the beaten egg and sugar.

Pour the mixture into 8 x 4 oz ramekins and place in a bain marie one-third full of water. Bake in the preheated oven for about 1 hour until just set. Remove and chill straight away.

When ready to serve, sprinkle the rest of the sugar evenly over the surface and caramelize under a very hot broiler, watching it carefully to make sure it does not burn. Serve as soon as the sugar has cooled and hardened.

BAKED NECTARINES

You could call this a cheat's dessert, so very easy is its preparation, but it looks glorious and tastes delicious. Be sure to serve with fine almond cookies.

SERVES
6

INGREDIENTS

- 9 nectarines
- 3 tbsp brandy
- ¼ cup soft brown sugar
- 1–1¼ cups raspberries
- ¼ cup almond flakes
- crème fraîche or Greek yogurt, for serving

METHOD

Preheat the oven to 400°F.

Cut the nectarines in half and remove the pits. Place on a baking sheet, cut side up, and sprinkle with the brandy and the sugar and add the raspberries. Scatter the almond flakes all over and bake in the preheated oven for 10 minutes.

Serve 3 halves per portion, with crème fraîche or Greek yogurt, and a fine almond cookie. The raspberries will have softened and dissolved in parts and, combined with the sugar and brandy, will make a sweet and tangy syrup for the nectarines.

BITTER CHOCOLATE MOUSSE TART

Use the best chocolate you can find. Most supermarkets now stock a European unsweetened dark chocolate with a 70–72 per cent cocoa solid content (as opposed to the usual 34 per cent), which is ideal for this tart. Any higher and the chocolate is pretty inedible by most standards.

INGREDIENTS

FOR THE TART SHELL
- 2 cups all purpose flour, sifted
- pinch of salt
- 6 tbsp sugar
- 2 egg yolks, medium sized, beaten
- ½ cup plus 2 tbsp unsalted butter, diced

FOR THE FILLING
- 11 oz (11 squares) bittersweet chocolate, broken into pieces
- 1 cup butter, cut into pieces
- 2 eggs, medium sized
- 4 egg yolks, medium sized
- 6 tbsp sugar

METHOD

To make the tart shell, mix together the flour, salt, and sugar in a bowl and make a well in the center. Put the egg yolks and butter in the well and, using your fingertips, first work the egg yolks into the butter, then work this mixture into the flour to form a smooth dough. Wrap in plastic wrap and refrigerate for 20 minutes.

Preheat the oven to 400°F.

Butter an 11 in loose-bottomed tart pan, then sprinkle 1 tbsp of flour over it and move it about to coat all over, shaking any excess flour out. Roll out the dough and line the pan with it. Prick the base with a fork and chill for 15 minutes. Then bake in the preheated oven for 15 minutes until pale gold in color.

Meanwhile, make the filling. Melt the chocolate with the butter; let cool. Whisk the whole eggs, yolks, and sugar with an electric beater for 5 minutes, until the mixture has doubled in volume and is pale, thick, and leaves a trail when the beaters are lifted. Gently pour in the melted chocolate and fold in carefully.

Pour the mixture into the tart shell and bake in the preheated oven for 8–10 minutes until just set, remembering that the mixture will become firmer once it has cooled down. Remove the tart from the pan, and ideally serve while just warm with chilled crème fraîche.

BAKED WINTER FRUIT

This is a sugar-free, guilt-free dessert that is nonetheless delicious and warming. It is also very simple to make and therefore ideal for when you are entertaining because it can be left to bake slowly in the oven while you attend to the rest of the meal. Don't bother with cooking apples, but do choose fruit with as much flavor as possible. You could add brown sugar if you like, sprinkled on at the end, just before the fruit goes under the broiler, where it will caramelize beautifully.

SERVES

6

INGREDIENTS

- 3 firm, green apples, large
- 3 pears, preferably Comice, just ripe
- 18 prunes, pitted
- 12–18 figs, dried but moist
- 18 soft dried apricots
- zest and juice of 1 orange

- ½ cup apple juice
- 1 small piece ginger, finely grated
- pinch of cinnamon
- ¼ cup almond flakes, toasted
- zest of 1 lime
- Greek yogurt, for serving

METHOD

Preheat the oven to 350°F.

Cut the unpeeled apples and pears into quarters, first removing the cores. Place in a large shallow glass or other ovenproof dish, and add the prunes, figs, and apricots. Mix with the orange and apple juice, ginger, and cinnamon. Cover with foil and place in the preheated oven for 1 hour.

When baked, remove the foil, stir the fruit around so it is well coated with juice, and place the dish under a hot broiler for a couple of minutes, so that the fruit just slightly chars in places. Garnish with the toasted almond flakes and orange and lime zest, reserving some of each to garnish the Greek yogurt. Serve hot or cold.

PINEAPPLE, RAISIN, AND COCONUT COBBLER

Cobbler sales at Cranks tripled the week this version appeared on the menu.

INGREDIENTS

- 2 lb pineapple (approximately 2 pineapples)
- 2 tbsp raw cane sugar
- 1¼ cups raisins
- ¼ cup desiccated coconut
- 1 tbsp rum or brandy
- 1 tsp finely chopped ginger
- 1 quantity cobbler mixture (see page 220)
- crème anglaise (see page 220) or heavy cream, for serving

METHOD

Peel the pineapple and cut into even-sized cubes. Place in a pan with all other ingredients except the cobbler mixture, and simmer gently for 5 minutes.

Preheat the oven to 400°F.

Pour the pineapple mixture into an ovenproof dish and sprinkle generously with the cobbler mixture. Don't press the mixture down or you will lose the desirable crumbly texture and end up with a hard crust instead. Bake in the preheated oven for 35 minutes, or until the cobbler is set in large lumps and very pale gold in color. Serve warm, with custard or heavy cream.

CHOCOLATE PECAN TART

I love the rich, sticky sweetness of pecan tart, and the decadent addition of chocolate makes this a dessert for times when sugar cravings are running at their highest. Served freshly out of the oven, still warm and with a dollop of homemade ice cream, or heavy cream, this is almost too rich to tackle at the end of a full meal. But reserved for a Sunday afternoon teatime with friends, oh bliss!

SERVES
8 – 1 0

INGREDIENTS

- ¾ cup sugar
- ½ cup butter
- 2 eggs, medium sized, beaten
- 1 tbsp cornstarch
- 2 cups pecan nuts, halved

- 4 oz (4 squares) unsweetened dark chocolate, broken into small pieces
- 1 tsp unsweetened cocoa, dissolved in 1 tsp cold water
- prebaked sweet pie shell (see page 222)

METHOD

Preheat the oven to 375°F.

Place the sugar and butter in a mixer bowl and beat until light and fluffy. Add the eggs, a little at a time, beating well after each addition. Fold in the cornstarch, three-quarters of the pecan nuts, the chocolate, and cocoa liquid until evenly blended.

Pour the mixture into the prebaked 12 in pie shell and decorate with the remaining pecans. Bake in the preheated oven for 40–45 minutes or until the filling has set. Serve warm with extra thick heavy cream or crème fraîche.

FRUIT SAVARIN

Savarin dough is very similar to brioche dough, but has twice as much milk and half as much butter. It is very lightly sweetened, hence its suitability for desserts like rum babas, when the dough is drenched with sugar syrup, and for this recipe where the finished savarin is soaked through with the juice of mixed berries. In fact, the juice needs to be spooned over for a good 10 minutes, so that it is thoroughly absorbed and the savarin becomes moist and bright red. Savarin dough must be used as soon as it is made. Once risen, it cannot be allowed to rest at all.

This recipe is based on one by the Roux brothers, and the poppyseeds were Suzanne Cullen's idea.

SERVES

6

INGREDIENTS

- ½ oz cake yeast or 2 tbsp dried yeast
- 1 cup warm milk
- 1 tsp salt
- 4 cups white bread flour, sifted
- 6 eggs, medium sized
- ¾ cup unsalted butter, softened
- 1 tbsp poppyseeds
- 1 tbsp sugar

FOR THE SYRUP

- 1½ cups juice from the frozen berries or water
- 1½ cups sugar

TO SERVE

- 4 cups frozen mixed berries, especially raspberries, defrosted, or 4 cups mixed fresh blackberries, raspberries, and blueberries
- ½ cup sugar
- 2 cups heavy cream, whipped

METHOD

Place the yeast and half the warm milk in a mixer bowl and beat lightly with a wire whisk, then add the salt. Add the flour, eggs, and butter and knead the dough using the mixer dough hook for about 10 minutes, until it is smooth and quite elastic. Now gradually add the remaining milk to obtain a supple dough which does not break when you stretch it between your fingers.

Place the dough in a bowl covered with a cloth and let rise for about 1 hour in a warm place or until it has doubled in volume. Punch down the dough by flipping it backward and forward between your hands a couple of times.

Brush the inside of a 10 in ring mold with softened butter and fill with the savarin dough. Allow to rise once more, this time in the pan, for about 40 minutes. Preheat the oven to 425°F and bake for 30 minutes. Unmold the savarin and return to the oven, placed on a baking sheet, for a further 5 minutes so that it is evenly browned all over. Place on a wire rack and let cool for 1 hour.

Meanwhile, make the syrup by placing the fruit juice or water and the sugar in a pan. Boil for 3 minutes and let cool.

Place the savarin upside down on the wire rack and place a plate underneath the rack. Poke holes all over the savarin with a skewer, and spoon the cooled syrup all over, catching the juices as they drip onto the plate and pouring them over again, until the sponge is well soaked.

Place on a serving plate. Mix the berries in the sugar and pile them in the middle and around the top. Pipe a circle of whipped cream around the outer edge. Serve any remaining cream separately.

CHOCOLATE AND WALNUT ROULADE

WITH RASPBERRIES

A festive-looking cake that takes about 30 minute to make and bake, but has all the richness, lightness, and sweetness you could wish for in a dessert

SERVES
10–12

INGREDIENTS

- 1 lb (16 squares) bittersweet chocolate
- 2 tsp instant coffee
- ¾ cup hot water
- 1¼ cups sugar
- 10 eggs, medium sized, separated
- 1 heaping tbsp coarsely ground walnuts

FOR THE FILLING

- 1½ cups heavy cream
- 1 cup fresh or frozen raspberries, defrosted
- confectioners' sugar, to decorate

METHOD

Preheat the oven to 375°F. Line an 11 x 17 in jelly roll pan with good quality brown paper.

Break the chocolate into small pieces and melt in a bowl placed on top of a saucepan of boiling water. Dissolve the coffee in the hot water, add to the melted chocolate, and mix well. Remove from the heat and set aside to cool.

Meanwhile, whisk the sugar and egg yolks until thick and fluffy so that when the whisk is lifted it leaves behind a trail which holds for a count of 5 seconds. Add the cooled chocolate to the egg and sugar mixture. Then whisk the egg whites until stiff, folding in the ground walnuts so they are evenly distributed in the mixture. Carefully fold the egg whites into the chocolate mixture. Pour onto the prepared baking sheet and bake in the preheated oven for 15–18 minutes. Check whether the mixture is set by inserting a skewer or the fine point of a knife into the cake and making sure it comes out clean. If not, return to the oven for a further 5 minutes or until set. Let cool in the pan.

While the roulade cools, whip the cream. Spread the roulade with the whipped cream, leaving a gap at both ends as it will spread outward as you roll the roulade, and gently cover with raspberries. Carefully roll up like a Swiss roll, using the paper to help you. Transfer to a long cake plate and dust with confectioners' sugar. Don't worry if the roulade cracks as you roll it as this adds to its character. It is best eaten immediately, but can be refrigerated for several hours.

PEAR AND BLACKBERRY COBBLER

Another ever-popular cobbler.

INGREDIENTS

CREME ANGLAISE

- 2 cups heavy cream
- 1 cup milk
- 1 vanilla pod
- 5 egg yolks, large
- 3 tbsp sugar
- 2 level tsp cornstarch

FOR THE COBBLER

- 3 cups white flour, sifted
- ¾ cup sugar
- 1 cup unsalted butter, cubed
- pinch of salt

FOR THE FILLING

- 3 lb pears, ripe but still firm, peeled, cored, and each cut into 6 slices
- ¼ cup sugar
- 1 lb fresh blackberries

METHOD

For the crème anglaise, place the cream and milk in a saucepan with the vanilla pod, bring to gently simmering. Remove from the heat and allow the vanilla pod to infuse for 10–15 minutes. Remove the pod and wipe it clean for further use (see page 209).

Meanwhile, whisk the egg yolks, sugar, and cornstarch together in a bowl, until thick and creamy. Add a little of the hot milk and cream mixture, stir well, and return the egg mixture to the pan. Heat again on gentle heat, whisking continuously until thickened. Immediately remove from the heat and place a piece of wax paper or plastic wrap over the surface to stop a skin forming. Refrigerate until needed.

Make the cobbler by mixing the flour and sugar together and add the cubed butter. Rub lightly with your fingers until the mixture turns to soft crumbs.

To make the filling, place the pears and the sugar in a saucepan and cook gently for 8 minutes until softened but still intact. Add the blackberries, stir, and remove from heat.

Preheat the oven to 400°F. Place the fruit in an ovenproof dish 12 x 8 in and cover with the cobbler. Bake in the preheated oven for 30–35 minutes until crisped and pale gold. Serve hot with crème anglaise.

LEMON PUDDING

A light and popular lemon dessert often served at Cranks. Lemon is always a favorite, but you could also use other citrus fruits. Experiment with tangerine, grapefruit, lime, and orange juices, alone or in combination.

INGREDIENTS

- ½ cup plus 2 tbsp unsalted butter
- 1½ cups raw cane sugar
- 6 eggs, medium sized, separated
- 1 cup white flour, sifted
- zest and juice of 2 lemons
- 3⅓ cups milk

METHOD

Preheat the oven to 350°F.

Cream the butter with three-quarters of the sugar until smooth and doubled in volume. Gradually add the egg yolks with a spoonful of the flour. Beat in the lemon zest and juice. Fold in the rest of the flour, alternating with the milk. Whisk the egg whites until stiff, then add the remaining sugar, and continue to whisk until glossy. Carefully fold into the lemon mixture, taking care not to over-mix or the egg whites will go flat.

Pour into an ovenproof dish 12 x 8 in and place in a bain marie. Bake in the preheated oven for 30–35 minutes until set.

PEAR, ALMOND, AND BLACKBERRY TART

If I could only ever eat one dessert again, this would have to be the one.

SERVES
10

INGREDIENTS

FOR THE SWEET PIE DOUGH
- 3 cups all purpose flour, sifted
- pinch of salt
- 1 cup cold unsalted butter, diced
- 1 cup confectioners' sugar
- 2 egg yolks

FOR THE FILLING
- 1 cup unsalted butter, softened
- 1 cup sugar

- 2 cups blanched whole almonds, ground
- 6 eggs, medium sized
- 5 ripe Comice pears, peeled, halved, and cored
- ¾ cup blackberries
- crème fraîche or mascarpone, for serving

TO GLAZE
- 1 tbsp apricot jam, dissolved in a little hot water (optional)

METHOD

To make the dough, place the sifted flour and salt on a clean, dry surface, and make a well in the center. Put the diced butter in the middle, then work with your fingertips until very soft. Sift the confectioners' sugar onto the butter and work it in until smooth. Add the egg yolks and mix well. Gradually draw in the flour and mix until smooth and amalgamated. Wrap the dough in plastic wrap and refrigerate for at least 1 hour.

Preheat the oven to 400°F. Butter and flour the sides and bottom of a 12 in loose-bottomed fluted tart pan, and roll the dough out on a well floured surface, then lift carefully into place. This may be quite difficult as the dough is so buttery. Alternatively, simply place the dough in the pan and press it evenly over the sides and bottom. Prick all over with a fork and bake blind for 20 minutes until pale gold. Remove from the oven and reduce the temperature to 350°F.

For the filling, cream the butter and sugar in a mixer until the mixture is pale and light. Add the ground almonds and blend for a few seconds. Then beat in the eggs one at a time. Place the pear halves face down in the tart shell and pour the almond mixture on top, making sure that some of the pear remains exposed. (You can 'fan' out the pears, by making slits in the flesh from top to bottom so they remain attached at one end.) Dot the blackberries evenly all over the surface in between the gaps. Bake for 35–40 minutes or until set. Very lightly brush with the thinned down apricot jam. Serve warm with crème fraîche or mascarpone.

CREPES WITH APPLES, CALVADOS, AND MAPLE SYRUP
SERVED WITH PECAN ICE CREAM

Crêpes are a little time-consuming to prepare, but they freeze well and can be easily thawed by steaming them in a dish set over a pan of boiling water. They have a hundred and one applications, both savory and sweet, and this is one of my favorites.

SERVES

6

INGREDIENTS

- 12 or more crêpes (see Gâteau de Crêpes Florentines on page 30 for recipe)

FOR THE FILLING

- 6 large fragrant apples
- 2 tbsp butter
- 1 tbsp soft brown sugar
- 4–5 tbsp maple syrup
- ¼ cup white marzipan (optional)
- ¾ cup almonds, roasted and roughly chopped

FOR THE SAUCE

- 2 tbsp butter
- 1 tbsp soft brown sugar
- 4 tbsp Calvados or brandy

METHOD

To make the filling, peel and core the apples, and cut into medium slices. Melt the butter in a pan, and add the apples and sugar. Cook gently over low heat for 10 minutes, until some of the apples have begun to dissolve and the rest are soft but intact. Add the maple syrup and stir gently. Add the marzipan, if using, and stir until it has dissolved. Finally, stir in the almonds.

Warm the crêpes and put a spoonful of the filling in the center of each. Fold the crêpes over to form small neat squares 2½ x 2½ in. Set aside and keep warm. Meanwhile, make the sauce by melting the butter, sugar, and Calvados or brandy together over low heat in a large, flat pan. Return the crêpes to the pan, moving them about gently so that they become coated in the sauce. Serve with Pecan Ice Cream (see page 225).

PECAN ICE CREAM

I usually make more ice cream than required for one sitting, and freeze it in two separate containers. If you have time, take the opportunity to make meringues with all the leftover egg whites (see page 203).

SERVES
10

INGREDIENTS

- 2 cups milk
- 7 cups heavy cream
- 15 egg yolks
- ¼ cup sugar
- ½ cup maple syrup
- 1 cup pecan nuts, half blended to a purée and the other half roughly chopped

METHOD

Place the milk and heavy cream in a heavy-bottomed saucepan. Heat until just below boiling point and set aside. With an electric mixer set at low speed, beat the egg yolks and sugar for 8–10 minutes until the mixture is pale and thick and leaves a ribbon trail behind when the beaters are lifted.

Pour a little of the warm cream into the egg and sugar mixture, mix well, and then return the whole lot to the pan set over low heat. Cook gently, stirring constantly with a wooden spoon to prevent the mixture from curdling, until the custard thickens and coats the back of the spoon. Strain immediately through a fine strainer into a bowl and stir in the maple syrup. Cool down, preferably by setting over a second bowl filled with ice. Finally, add the pecan purée and the chopped pecans, and stir well so they don't all sink to the bottom.

Either place in an ice cream machine until frozen or place in a suitable freezer container. With the latter, remove the ice cream from the freezer after a couple of hours, before it is frozen solid, and whisk in an electric mixer until any ice crystals are broken down. Return to the freezer, and repeat this procedure one more time before allowing the ice cream to freeze fully.

CHRISTMAS PUDDING

I have made several changes to the traditional Cranks Christmas Pudding. Among other things, I have added more almonds, the zest and juice of 1 orange, grated apple, and a touch of cinnamon. The quantities here are for two puddings.

SERVES 16

INGREDIENTS

- 2 tbsp butter for greasing
- ½ cup fresh soft white bread crumbs
- 6 tbsp wholewheat flour
- 6 tbsp white flour
- ¾ cup unsalted butter or vegetarian suet
- 3 eggs, medium sized, beaten
- 1¼ cups currants
- 1¼ cups raisins
- 1¼ cups golden raisins
- ½ apple, unpeeled and grated
- zest and juice of 1 orange
- ½ cup almonds, roughly chopped
- 1 cup raw brown sugar

- ½ tsp allspice
- ¼ tsp ground nutmeg
- ¼ tsp ground cinnamon
- ¼ tsp salt
- 1 tbsp orange marmalade
- ¾ cup sherry or brandy

BRANDY SAUCE
- 2 cups heavy cream
- ½–¾ cup confectioners' sugar
- 1 tbsp cornstarch mixed with 1 tbsp milk
- 6 tbsp brandy

METHOD

Grease two 2 lb pudding molds with melted butter. Cut 2 large circles of wax paper so they overlap the tops of the pudding molds by about 4 in. Combine all the ingredients together in a large mixing bowl and stir well until evenly mixed. Press the mixture into the molds. Brush the paper circle with more melted butter and press down onto the surface of the pudding so it is completely sealed in. Secure with string. Finally, cover with a piece of foil. Place in a large pan filled with water, and steam, making sure that the water reaches halfway up the sides of the pudding molds at all times (a pressure cooker is ideal) and add more boiling water if necessary. It is also possible to cook the puddings in a bain marie set in the oven on 300°F. Check the water levels as above.

Before serving, steam for a further 2 hours in the same fashion, then unmold the puddings, baste with a little warm brandy, and set alight. Serve with brandy butter or brandy sauce.

To make the brandy sauce, put the cream and sugar in a saucepan, bring to a boil, then lower the heat and reduce gently by a quarter. Stir in the cornstarch and boil for a further minute. Keep the sauce hot without boiling and then, just before serving, add the brandy and stir well.

STICKY DATE PUDDING
WITH BRANDY AND PECAN SAUCE

Not a dessert for the faint-hearted, this is as rich and gooey as they come.

SERVES
6 – 8

INGREDIENTS

- 1¼ cups dates, pitted and soaked in boiling water for 20 minutes
- 1¼ cups white organic self-rising flour
- 1 tsp baking powder
- 4 eggs, medium sized
- 6 tbsp butter, melted and cooled
- ¾ cup light brown sugar
- 1¼ cups fresh soft white bread crumbs
- 1 tsp vanilla extract
- 1½ cups warm water
- heavy cream, to serve

FOR THE SAUCE

- ½ cup water
- ¾ cup light brown sugar
- 6 tbsp unsalted butter
- 1 cup brandy
- ½ cup pecans, lightly toasted

METHOD

Roughly chop the dates. Sift the flour and baking powder into a mixing bowl. Add the eggs, softened butter, sugar, bread crumbs, and half the chopped dates and, using an electric mixer, whisk all the ingredients together, slowly adding the vanilla extract and water until the mixture is smooth. Fold in the rest of the dates.

Transfer the mixture either to 8 individual 6 oz buttered pudding molds, or to one large 2 lb one. Cover the tops securely with foil and steam for 2 hours, either in a large pan with the water reaching half way up the sides, or in a bain marie tray set in the oven heated to 350°F, with the water reaching halfway up the sides. For both methods, add more boiling water if the level goes down.

Remove when firm and springy to the touch. Run a small pointed knife around the edges and invert onto a serving plate.

To make the sauce, place the water, sugar, and butter in a pan. Bring to a boil, reduce the heat, and simmer for 2 minutes, adding the brandy toward the end and whisking with a small hand whisk. At the last minute, fold in the toasted pecans.

Spoon the sauce over the steamed puddings and serve with the heavy cream.

SUMMER PUDDING

Seasonality not being what it used to be, there is no reason why you shouldn't make this pudding with frozen berries as well as with fresh ones so you can enjoy it all year round. In winter you may like to warm the frozen berries to allow the juices to soak through more easily with no need for overnight refrigeration. You could even sprinkle it with a little extra sugar and give the pudding a quick blast under a hot broiler. Rolling the slices of bread that are to line the dish with a rolling pin helps them to stay in place. The remaining slices can stay as they are.

SERVES
8–10

INGREDIENTS

- 1½ loaves white sliced bread, crusts removed
- 2 lb mixed summer berries
- 1 cup soft brown sugar
- crème fraîche or heavy cream, for serving
- cinnamon and mint leaves, to decorate

METHOD

Line a rectangular 10 x 8 in ovenproof dish with 10 slices of the bread. Reserve a couple of tablespoons of the berries for decoration (if using fresh) and mix the rest with the sugar. Place one-third of them over the first layer of bread. Add a second layer of sliced bread. Add more berries so that no white shows through. Repeat one more time, finishing off with a layer of bread. Weigh down the pudding with another dish or other appropriate weights. Refrigerate overnight weighted down in this fashion, so that all the bread is well soaked through with berries and juice.

Serve with crème fraîche or heavy cream, lightly sprinkled with cinnamon. Decorate with a couple of fresh mint leaves, and the reserved berries, and serve.

DAIRY-FREE CHOCOLATE CAKE
WITH RASPBERRIES

You do need to use a good quality bittersweet dark chocolate for the frosting, though it does not need to be as high in cocoa content as for other recipes. A sweeter chocolate works better because of the baking soda in the cake, which can otherwise leave a slightly salty aftertaste.

SERVES
10

INGREDIENTS

- ¾ cup espresso coffee
- 6 tbsp water
- 6 tbsp vegetable margarine
- 6 tbsp sugar
- 1 tbsp corn syrup
- 1¾ cups all purpose unbleached white flour, sifted
- 1 tsp baking soda
- ¼ cup unsweetened cocoa
- 4 tbsp soy milk
- ½ tsp vanilla extract

FOR THE FROSTING

- 3 oz (3 squares) bittersweet chocolate
- 3 tbsp vegetable margarine
- 4 tbsp water
- 2 cups confectioners' sugar

FOR THE TOPPING

- 1 cup frozen or fresh raspberries
- 3 tbsp sugar

METHOD

Preheat the oven to 350°F. Grease and line an 8 in layer pan with baking parchment.

Put the coffee, water, margarine, sugar, and syrup in a pan and heat, stirring until the sugar dissolves. Simmer for 5 minutes. Whisk in the dry ingredients until well blended. Stir in the soy milk and vanilla extract.

Pour into the prepared pan and bake in the preheated oven for 25 minutes, or until set. Slice into 2 even layers and let cool on a wire rack.

To make the frosting, place the chocolate, margarine, and water in a dish or pan set over a saucepan of boiling water until melted. Stir well until amalgamated and sift in the confectioners' sugar, beating the mixture until smooth. Let cool slightly, then spread some onto one half of the cake and sandwich together with the other half. Spread the remaining frosting all over the top and sides.

For the topping, place the raspberries in a pan with the sugar and heat very gently until the sugar has dissolved and the raspberries are just beginning to break up. Let cool slightly, then spoon over the center of the cake only, leaving a surrounding area of cake uncovered. The cake is best eaten very fresh or even slightly warm.

PASSION FRUIT CHEESECAKE

If there is a more delicious cheesecake out there, I'd like to know what it is! The passion fruit in the filling and the lime zest and coconut in the dough make this just the most delicious cheesecake ever.

SERVES
10–12

INGREDIENTS

FOR THE BASE

- 1¾ cups Graham crackers, crushed
- ½ cup butter, at room temperature
- zest of 1 lime
- 1 tbsp unsweetened coconut flakes, chopped
- 1 tbsp ground almonds

FOR THE FILLING

- 1 cup farmers cheese or fromage blanc
- 1¾ cups cream cheese, softened
- 3 eggs, medium sized
- 1 cup heavy cream
- 6 passion fruit
- ½ cup sugar

METHOD

Preheat the oven to 350°F. Line a 10 in springform pan with a circle of parchment paper.

Combine the crushed Graham crackers with the butter, lime zest, and coconut. Mix thoroughly. Then roll into a ball, dust with the ground almonds, and work in so the mixture is slightly firmer and easily manageable. Press the Graham cracker mixture evenly into the bottom of the pan and set aside.

Mix the farmers cheese and cream cheese with 2 whole eggs and the yolk of the third. Reserve the final egg white. Whip the cream and fold into the cream cheese mixture. Cut the passion fruits in half and scoop out the flesh and seeds. Put in a strainer held over the cheesecake mixture. Press through the juice and fold in, then, separately, fold in the seeds. Whisk the remaining egg white with the sugar until it stands in soft peaks, and fold in. Pour over the Graham cracker base. Bake for 1 hour or until just set, making sure the top does not brown. Allow to cool on a wire rack. Release from the springform pan. Serve cold or at room temperature.

BREAD AND
BUTTER PUDDING

Much of the culinary revival in British food has been led by the wealth of recipes in the category of sticky, gooey, comfort desserts. No other country seems to produce these hot, filling, meal-after-a-meal, wicked concoctions. As a child, my mother would refer to them as Les Puddings Anglais and, no matter what they were called, we loved them. The passage of time has not diminished my fondness for them either.

SERVES
8 – 10

INGREDIENTS

- 4 tbsp butter, plus 2 tbsp for the apples (optional)
- ¾ cup soft brown sugar, plus 3 tbsp
- 3 cooking apples, peeled and sliced
- 1¼ cups raisins
- ¼ cup brandy
- 6 eggs, medium sized
- ¾ cup heavy cream
- 2 cups milk
- ½ tsp cinnamon
- 8 slices day-old white bread, crusts left on, and sliced

METHOD

Melt 2 tbsp of the butter in a saucepan, add 2 tbsp of the sugar, and gently cook the apple slices for 6–7 minutes or until they are tender. Set aside. Soak the raisins in the brandy for 20 minutes.

Preheat the oven to 350°F. Butter a 10 x 8 in ovenproof dish. Mix the eggs and all but 2 tbsp of the remaining sugar with an electric hand-held mixer, and add the cream, milk, and most of the cinnamon.

Butter the bread on one side only and cut each slice across into 2 triangles. Place half the bread, butter side up, in the bottom of the ovenproof dish. Then scatter with half the raisins and half the apple, and place the remaining bread slices on top. Cut the sandwiches in half and overlap so they are standing almost upright. Scatter with the remaining raisins and apple, and pour the egg and cream mixture all over. Sprinkle with a little more cinnamon and 2 tbsp of sugar. Place in the preheated oven and bake for 35 minutes or until the top layer of bread is crunchy and golden and the custard is just set.

If you wish, finish off the pudding by placing under a hot broiler for 2 minutes to caramelize the sugar.

cakes and

baking

Cakes are popular teatime treats,
and in this chapter you'll find the old favorites like
carrot cake and date slices, plus exciting new ideas
such as orange parsnip cake, pear tarte tatin, and
polenta and ricotta cake.

For a very long time, all the cakes at Cranks were made with only wholewheat flour. This certainly created a new style of baking, which went some way toward making the health-conscious feel less guilty about eating cakes. Some of these recipes were successful and even seemed to benefit from being made with wholewheat flour: Carrot cake is a good example. But, there are definitely some recipes that require the more delicate texture of white flour.

Many of the recipes in this chapter are well suited to afternoon teas, especially in the winter when you feel the need for a comforting slice of something sweet to brighten a dull day. There are also foolproof recipes for baking your own breads, scones and brioche.

Whatever the occasion, eat cake, enjoy to your heart's content, and never, ever, feel even the tiniest bit guilty.

ORANGE PARSNIP CAKE

It may not seem obvious, but it makes perfect sense to use parsnips in a dessert. They are naturally full of sugar, and lend themselves as well to baking as their obvious cousin, the carrot of the by now legendary Carrot Cake (see page 238).

SERVES

8

INGREDIENTS

- ½ cup butter, cut into cubes
- 2 tsp grated orange zest
- ¼ cup soft brown sugar
- 3 tbsp orange juice
- 3 eggs, medium sized
- ½ cup plus 2 tbsp self-rising flour

- ½ cup, plus 2 tbsp wholewheat flour
- ¾ tsp baking powder
- pinch of salt
- ½ lb parsnips, finely grated
- 1 prebaked sweet pie shell (see page 222)
- crème fraîche for serving

METHOD

Preheat the oven to 400°F. Cream the butter, orange zest, and sugar with an electric hand-held mixer until pale yellow. Add the orange juice and beat in the eggs, one at a time. Fold in the flours, baking powder, salt, and grated parsnip. Pour the mixture into the prebaked pie shell and bake in the preheated oven for 1 hour or until firm to the touch. Serve with crème fraîche.

CARROT CAKE

Carrot cake is as much a part of the fabric of Cranks as Homity Pie and Cheese Scones (see pages 108 and 246). Try removing any of them from the menu and there is an outcry. Customers threaten never to return and staff are up in arms. Cranks has come a long way, but these signature recipes hold an almost hallowed place.

SERVES

8

INGREDIENTS

- ½ lb carrots
- 2 eggs, medium sized
- ¼ cup raw brown sugar
- 6 tbsp corn oil
- 1 cup wholewheat flour
- 1½ tsp baking powder

- ½ tsp salt
- 1 tsp ground cinnamon
- ½ tsp ground nutmeg
- 2 heaping tbsp dried shredded coconut
- ⅓ cup raisins

METHOD

Grease and line the base of a 7 in square cake pan with parchment paper. Preheat the oven to 375°F.

Finely grate the carrots. Whisk the eggs and sugar together until thick and creamy. Whisk in the oil slowly, then add the remaining ingredients, and mix together to combine evenly. Spoon the mixture into the prepared pan. Level the surface and bake in the preheated oven for 20–25 minutes, until firm to the touch and golden brown. Cool on a wire rack. For best results, serve while still warm.

POLENTA AND RICOTTA CAKE

WITH APRICOTS AND BRANDY

This is a lovely, easy-to-eat cake made with two typically Italian ingredients. I've added the apricots to lighten the rich texture with a gentle tanginess. The brandy is a wicked note in an otherwise rather virtuous cake.

SERVES
8 – 10

INGREDIENTS

- 1¼ cups soft, dried apricots, sliced
- 5 tbsp apricot or ordinary brandy
- 2 cups polenta (not the instant type)
- 2 cups self-rising flour
- 1 rounded tsp baking powder
- 1 cup sugar
- 1 cup very fresh ricotta

- ½ cup butter, melted
- 1 cup tepid water
- ½ cup walnuts, chopped
- 1 level tbsp brown sugar
- 1 tbsp apricot jam dissolved in boiling water, to glaze
- 1 cup mascarpone cheese, to serve

METHOD

Place the sliced apricots in a bowl with the brandy and allow the flavors to develop for at least 15 minutes.

Preheat the oven to 325°F. Line a 9 in springform pan with wax paper.

Sift the polenta, flour, and baking powder into a large bowl and tip the polenta grains left in the sieve into the bowl. Add the sugar, ricotta, melted butter, and water and whisk with an electric hand-held whisk for about 1 minute until well blended. Fold in the nuts, apricots, and brandy. Spoon the mixture into the prepared pan and smooth the surface with the back of a spoon. Scatter the brown sugar evenly over the surface. Bake on the middle shelf of the preheated oven for 1–1½ hours, or until the cake springs back when gently pressed in the middle. Cover the top with foil for the first 30 minutes.

Leave the baked cake in its pan for 15 minutes, then release from the springform pan and allow to cool on a wire rack. Glaze with the apricot jam and serve with the mascarpone.

PEAR TARTE TATIN

For many years, tarte tatin was one thing and one thing only: An upside-down apple pie made famous by the Tatin sisters who invented it. Recently though, the name Tatin has been applied to any and every combination of fruit and vegetables as long as they are baked upside-down and inverted before serving. Pears work really well because of their high sugar content which aids their caramelization. Don't be tempted to use under-ripe pears, as no amount of cooking will substitute for their natural sugars and flavors when ripe.

SERVES

8

INGREDIENTS

- 1 cup unsalted butter
- 1 cup raw cane sugar
- 6 firm, ripe pears, peeled, cored, and quartered
- ½ lb ready-made puff pastry

METHOD

Preheat the oven to 425°F.

Melt the butter and sugar together in a saucepan over gentle heat. When they start to caramelize, add the pear quarters. Cook, turning over regularly, until the pears start to brown. Place the cooked pears close together and face up in an 8 in layer pan, and pour over the excess caramel. Roll out the dough slightly larger than the pan, and place over the pears, tucking in the edges.

Bake in the preheated oven for about 20 minutes or until the crust is crisp and brown. Serve warm with crème anglaise (see page 220), pouring cream, mascarpone cheese, or pecan ice cream (see page 225).

DATE AND FIG LOG

This is easy to make, good for you, and dairy-free. It is delicious as it is, served with an orange and brandy sauce, or use the mixture as a filling for deep-fried sweet wontons (see page 24), served with the same sauce. It is also excellent served with vanilla ice cream. Good quality coconut flakes can be bought from well-stocked health food shops and are preferable to the usual packets of coconut flakes.

SERVES

6

INGREDIENTS

- 1¼ cups dates (mejdool are best)
- 1¼ cups soft dried figs
- 3 tbsp marsala wine
- 1 cup coconut flakes, two-thirds chopped and the remainder left whole
- ½ cup whole almonds, roughly chopped
- ½ tsp fresh grated ginger (optional)

FOR THE SAUCE

- ½ cup butter
- ½ cup plus 2 tbsp sugar
- zest and juice of 3 oranges
- zest and juice of 1 lemon
- 3 tbsp Grand Marnier or Cointreau
- 4 tbsp brandy

METHOD

Pit the dates and remove the stems from the figs. Place on a board and chop vigorously into small pieces. Transfer to a bowl and add the wine, coconut flakes, chopped almonds and ginger, if using. Mix well with your hands and shape into a log.

To make the sauce, place the butter and sugar in a saucepan and melt over gentle heat. Add the orange and lemon zest and juice, and stir for 1 minute. Add the orange liqueur and brandy, and continue to simmer for 2–3 minutes.

To serve, cut the log into ½ in slices and dip into the sauce, gently turning until well coated. Serve with a pool of sauce and vanilla ice cream.

The date and fig log can be served immediately, or wrap in plastic wrap and refrigerate until needed.

CHOCOLATE CAKE
WITH VIOLET CREME FRAICHE

I sometimes glaze the cake and serve while it is still just warm. If you cannot find violets, garnish with strips of candied orange peel.

SERVES
10–12

INGREDIENTS

- I cup butter, softened
- 2 cups sugar
- 6 eggs, medium sized
- 8 oz (8 squares) bittersweet chocolate, melted and cooled
- 2 cups almonds, ground
- 2 cups fresh soft white bread crumbs

FOR THE FROSTING

- 6 oz (6 squares) bittersweet chocolate, broken into small pieces

- I tbsp clear honey
- 6 tbsp butter

FOR THE CREME FRAICHE

- I cup crème fraîche
- 2 cups sugar
- I bunch violets
- 2 egg whites, lightly beaten

METHOD

Line a 10 in layer pan with parchment paper. Grease with butter and dust lightly with unbleached flour. Preheat the oven to 375°F.

Cut the softened butter into small pieces and place in the bowl of an electric mixer. Add the sugar and beat with a whisk attachment on the highest setting until pale and creamy. Add one egg at a time, waiting for each to be well incorporated before adding the next. Do not be alarmed if this looks curdled, it will come back together again as soon as you pour in the melted chocolate. Slowly add the melted chocolate into the egg and sugar mixture. Slowly fold in the ground almonds and then the soft bread crumbs. Pour into the pan and bake for 40–45 minutes, or until firm.

Meanwhile, make the chocolate frosting. Melt the broken chocolate, honey, and butter in a bowl set over a pan of boiling water. When they have melted, stir well with a metal spoon until smooth. Put the still warm cake on a wire rack set over a plate and pour over the frosting. For the crème fraîche, fold 1 tbsp of sugar into the crème fraîche. Then separate the violet flowerheads from their stems, opening them out gently. Using a fine paint brush, coat each petal on both sides with lightly beaten egg white. Lightly sprinkle sugar from a teaspoon so that it sticks to the egg white. Place each flowerhead on a wire rack covered with paper towels until the egg white has dried and the sugar hardened. Decorate both the cake and the crème fraîche with the crystallized petals. Serve at once.

LEMON, LIME, AND POPPYSEED TRICKLE CAKE

This is a combination of two old-time favorites, the lemon cake and the poppyseed cake. You can bake it either in a loaf pan or a square pan, but the crucial thing is to drench it in lemon syrup so that it is moist and fragrant with a fine coating of frosting on top.

INGREDIENTS

- ½ cup butter, cut into pieces
- 2 tsp lime zest
- 2 tsp lemon zest
- 2 cups sugar
- 3 eggs, medium sized
- 2 cups self-rising flour, sifted
- 1 tbsp poppyseeds
- ½ cup plain yogurt

FOR THE SYRUP
- 4 tbsp lime juice
- 4 tbsp lemon juice
- 4 tbsp sugar

FOR THE DECORATION
- 4 tbsp sugar
- 3 tbsp lemon zest
- 3 tbsp lime zest

METHOD

Preheat the oven to 350°F. Line a 12 in loaf pan with wax paper, then butter and flour it.

Place the butter and the lime and lemon zest in the large mixing bowl of an electric mixer, and beat until light and creamy. Add the sugar gradually, and beat well after each addition. Beat in the eggs one at a time and mix well. Fold in the flour, poppyseeds, and the yogurt, spoonful by spoonful, alternating between the three. Spoon into the prepared loaf pan and bake in the preheated oven for 30–35 minutes until a skewer inserted into the center comes out clean. Let stand in the pan for about 5 minutes, then invert onto a wire rack.

To make the syrup, place the juices and the sugar in a pan. Simmer gently and stir continually, until the sugar dissolves, and then bring to a boil, this time without stirring, and boil for 3 minutes. Make holes all over the top of the cake with a fork, and pour the hot syrup over the hot cake. For the decoration, melt the sugar in a pan without stirring until the sugar dissolves and begins to go golden brown. Add the lemon and lime zest, and stir until coated and caramelized. Carefully lift out the zest with a fork and arrange all over the cake.

SCONES

The scones at Cranks are big generous things and we sell about 1500 of them a week. We use an organic wholewheat flour, and they are made daily by our night bakers. If you can bear to play around with something so quintessentially English, you could always add some contemporary tidbits. Try dried cherries or cranberries in sweet scones, or sundried tomatoes, black olives, red onion, or even pumpkin for the cheese scones.

SWEET SCONES

SERVES

6

INGREDIENTS

- 2 cups wholewheat self-rising flour, sifted
- pinch of salt
- 6 tbsp butter
- 2 tbsp raw brown sugar
- ½ cup golden raisins
- ½ cup milk

METHOD

Preheat the oven to 425°F.

Place the flour and a pinch of salt into a bowl. Rub in the butter until the mixture resembles fine crumbs. Stir in the sugar and golden raisins, then add almost all of the milk to obtain a soft, manageable dough. You may need slightly more or slightly less milk than given. Add more milk if necessary.

Knead the dough on a lightly floured surface, then roll out to about ¾ in thick. Use a 3 in cutter to stamp out the scones. Place about 1 in apart on a lightly greased baking sheet, and bake in the preheated oven for 10–15 minutes until golden. Cool on a wire rack. Serve with strawberry jam and clotted or whipped cream.

CHEESE SCONES

INGREDIENTS

- 4 cups wholewheat flour, sifted
- 3 tbsp baking powder
- large pinch of salt
- large pinch of cayenne pepper

- 4 tbsp butter
- 2 cups Cheddar cheese, shredded
- 1¼ cups milk

METHOD

Preheat the oven to 400°F.

Put the flour, baking powder, salt, and cayenne pepper in a bowl. Rub in the butter until the mixture resembles fine crumbs. Stir in most of the cheese and sufficient milk to obtain a soft, easy-to-handle dough. Knead gently, then roll out on a lightly floured surface to a thickness of 1 in. Stamp out 3 in rounds with a fluted cutter and place on a lightly greased baking sheet. Brush with milk and sprinkle with the remaining cheese. Bake in the preheated oven for about 20 minutes until golden. Cool on a wire rack and eat as soon as possible.

BRIOCHE

Brioche is that delicious slightly sweet, light, eggy bread that the French eat for breakfast with café au lait. If you don't possess a brioche pan, a round layer pan will do. Simply line it with wax paper twice as high as the pan. Always use bread flour when making brioche or other yeasted bread and cake yeast whenever possible. If you want to mix the dough by hand, triple the mixing times given in the recipe. This is not a recipe to attempt unless you have plenty of time: Note the double rising times.

INGREDIENTS

- ¾ oz cake yeast
- 6 tbsp warmed milk
- I tsp salt
- 3½ cups self-rising flour
- 3 eggs, medium sized

- 6 tbsp butter
- I tbsp sugar
- I egg yolk, to glaze
- I tsp milk, to glaze

METHOD

Whisk the yeast and milk lightly with a wire whisk and add the salt. Put the flour in a mixer bowl and make a well in the center. Into this break the eggs and add the yeast and milk mixture. Beat with a dough hook for 10 minutes until the dough is elastic.

Soften the butter and beat it with the sugar. Slowly add this to the dough, beating continuously on a low setting. Mix for a further 5 minutes, until the dough looks smooth and feels elastic. Cover with a dishcloth and leave in a warm place for 1½ hours, or until the dough has risen to at least twice its original volume. Lightly knead again 5–6 times. Tip the dough out onto a floured surface and shape into a large ball. For a traditional brioche shape, cut off a quarter of the dough. Shape the larger piece into a ball and place in a 1 quart brioche mold. Press a hole in the center with floured fingertips. Shape the remaining piece like an egg and fit the narrow end into the hole. Beat the egg yolk and milk together and use this to glaze the brioche. Brush over the top, with upward movements, to prevent the glaze from dripping down the sides, which would make the brioche stick to the pan.

Leave to rise in a warm place for a further 1½ hours, until almost doubled in size. Lightly glaze once more. Preheat the oven to 450°F, and bake the brioche for 40 minutes, until firm and golden. Unmold instantly and cool on a wire rack.

DUTCH APPLE PIE

I have been making this apple pie for years, and like it so much I've never bothered with another. As with all pie recipes, the secret lies in the short thin pie dough, but roll the dough a bit thicker for the braided top.

INGREDIENTS

- 4½ lb fragrant apples
- 4 tbsp butter
- 1 cup soft brown sugar
- pinch of cinnamon

- double quantity pie dough (see page 208)
- 1 heaping tbsp apricot jam, mixed with a little boiling water

METHOD

Preheat the oven to 400°F.

Peel and slice the apples no thicker than ¼ in. Melt the butter in a saucepan and add the sugar (reserving 1 tbsp for later use), the apple slices, and cinnamon. Cook on a low heat for 10–15 minutes until some of the apple has broken up, but most is still intact. Remove from the heat and drain off any excess liquid.

Generously butter a 12 in loose-bottomed pan and lightly sprinkle with flour, tapping gently to coat the pan evenly.

Roll out two-thirds of the dough no thicker than ⅛ in. Lift onto a rolling pin and lower into the pan, pressing well into the sides, and leaving a ½ in overhang. Prick all over with a fork and bake in the preheated oven for 15 minutes.

Roll out the remaining dough and cut into 8 strips ½ in wide, making sure the strips are long enough to go across the pan at its widest point. Also cut one extra long strip to go around the circumference.

Add the cooked apples to the prebaked pie shell. Make a lattice of the dough strips, weaving them over and under each other. Trim any overhanging pieces and cover the edges with the long strip of dough. "Flute" the edge by pinching this strip between your thumb and forefinger. Lightly sprinkle with the reserved brown sugar and bake for 20–25 minutes until golden brown. Immediately glaze with the apricot jam and serve hot or warm with crème fraîche or vanilla ice cream.

CRANKS WHOLEWHEAT BREAD

No Cranks cookery book would be complete without a recipe for this wholewheat bread. I know people who will make journeys of great lengths to procure a loaf of it. You may add herbs or seeds to the basic mixture. Do not be alarmed by the absence of kneading in the method: That's how it's meant to be.

MAKES

1 LOAF

OR

6 BAPS

INGREDIENTS

- ½ oz cake yeast
- 1 tsp Barbados sugar
- 1¼–1¾ cups warm water

- 1 tsp sea salt
- 4 cups organic wholewheat flour

METHOD

Lightly grease a 2 lb loaf pan. Mix the yeast and sugar in a small bowl with ³/₄ cup of the warm water. Leave in a warm place for 10 minutes to froth up. Combine the salt and flour on a clean work surface. Add the yeast mixture. Gradually add the rest of the water and mix well with your hands.

Place the dough in the prepared loaf pan. Put the pan in a warm place, cover with a dish cloth and allow to rise for about 20 minutes or until the dough is within ½ in of the top of the pan.

Preheat the oven to 400°F and bake the loaf for 35–40 minutes. Let cool for a few minutes then invert onto a wire rack.

To make buns, roll out the dough thickly on a lightly floured surface and stamp out six 4 in rounds. Place on a baking sheet and brush lightly with milk. Leave in a warm place to rise for 10–15 minutes. Bake at the above temperature for 20–25 minutes. Cool on a wire rack and eat as fresh as possible.

PUMPKIN PIE

I love vegetables that can be used in sweet as well as savory recipes, and pumpkin has always been a favorite. This is best in the fall, when pumpkins are abundant and huge as well as just the deep orange color that is required. This recipe is lighter than most, an effect achieved by whisking the egg whites and folding them in.

It is delicious served hot, and even more delicious when accompanied by lime and coconut ice cream (see page 205). Heavy cream is pretty good, too.

SERVES
8–10

INGREDIENTS

- 1½ lb pumpkin, peeled
- 1½ cups sugar or soft pale brown sugar
- 6 eggs, medium sized, separated
- good pinch of cinnamon
- pinch of freshly grated nutmeg
- 4 cardamom pods, seeds removed and pounded in a pestle and mortar
- 1 cup double cream
- 3 tbsp butter, melted
- 1 tsp cornstarch
- prebaked pie shell (see page 208)

METHOD

Preheat the oven to 350°F.

Cut the peeled pumpkin into 1 in chunks and steam for 10 minutes, or until tender.

Place the sugar, egg yolks, and spices in a bowl and mix well. Blend the pumpkin in a blender, or mash it with a potato masher until smooth, then add the egg yolk mixture, cream and melted butter. Whisk the egg whites with the cornstarch until stiff, and carefully fold into the pumpkin mixture. Pour into the pie shell and bake in the preheated oven for 50 minutes, or until set. Serve hot, warm, or cold.

PRUNE AND HONEY CAKE

An intensely flavored cake which has always sold very well at Cranks. You could substitute a fine wholewheat flour for half the white flour if you wish.

SERVES

8

INGREDIENTS

- 3 eggs, medium sized
- I cup soft brown sugar
- I cup corn oil
- ¾ cup milk
- 2¼ cups white flour, sifted
- ½ tsp baking soda
- ½ tsp cinnamon
- pinch of nutmeg

- ½ tsp ground cloves (optional)
- ½ tsp mixed spice
- 1¼ cups prunes, soaked, pitted, and chopped
- 3 tbsp Armagnac

FOR THE GLAZE

- 4 tbsp clear honey, lightly warmed

METHOD

Preheat the oven to 375°F. Butter and flour a 8 in round pan.

Place the eggs and sugar in a mixer bowl and whisk until pale and fluffy. Add the oil and milk, and continue to whisk until amalgamated. Now add the flour, baking soda, and the spices, and fold in gently. Lastly, fold in the prunes and Armagnac.

Transfer to the prepared pan and bake in the preheated oven for 45–60 minutes or until a thin skewer inserted in the middle comes out clean. Remove from the oven and leave in the pan for 15 minutes, then invert onto a plate.

Make holes over the top of the cake with a fork. Pour the warmed, runny honey all over the cake, and serve warm with whipped cream.

DATE SLICES

Date slices are another faithful Cranks standby, and rumor has it that they're slightly addictive. You can cut them into smaller pieces than the ones served in the restaurants, and serve them with tea. We use wholewheat flour but I have made it quite successfully with unbleached white flour. This is a perfect winter dessert with cream. You could also add a peeled, chopped apple to the dates for a lighter filling.

SERVES
6 – 8

INGREDIENTS

- 2½ cups dates, pitted
- 1 cup butter, cubed
- 2 cups wholewheat flour
- ¾ cup soft brown sugar
- 1 cup oats

METHOD

Steam the dates over a pan of boiling water for 10 minutes until softened, then loosely mash with a fork, and set aside. Preheat the oven to 400°F.

Rub the butter into the flour until it resembles fine bread crumbs, and add the sugar. Add the oats and mix in lightly. Pack half the mixture down tightly into an 8 in square ovenproof dish or pan, and cover with the date mixture. Spoon the remaining oat mixture on top of the dates, so it resembles a rough crumble. Bake in the preheated oven for 30 minutes. Let cool or serve warm.

INDEX *Alphabetical listing of recipes is in italic*